the art of ritual

the art of ritual

Creating and Performing Ceremonies for Growth and Change

Renee Beck and Sydney Barbara Metrick

CELESTIAL ARTS
Berkeley | Toronto

Celestial Arts
P.O. Box 7123
Berkeley, California 94707
www.tenspeed.com

Distributed in Australia by Simon & Schuster Australia, in Canada by Ten Speed Press Canada, in New Zealand by Southern Publishers Group, in South Africa by Real Books, and in the United Kingdom and Europe by Airlift Book Company.

Cover design by Melissa Ehn at Wilsted & Taylor Publishing Services
Text design by Mary Beth Salmon

Library of Congress Cataloging-in-Publication Data

Beck, Renee, 1951–
  The art of ritual : creating and performing ceremonies for growth and change / Renee Beck and Sydney Barbara Metrick.—Rev. ed.
      p. cm.
Includes bibliographical references and index.
  ISBN 1-58761-190-2
  1. Rites and ceremonies. 2. Spiritual life. I. Metrick, Sydney Barbara, 1947- II. Title.
  BL600.B435 2003
  203'.8—dc22

                        2003015401

Printed in Canada
First printing this edition, 2003

1 2 3 4 5 6 7 8 9 10—07 06 05 04 03

dedication

To Roie Beck, who instilled in me a great wonderment for ritual, God, and mystery.

—Renee Beck

To my oldest and dearest friend, Hank Matthews, who always has me focus on the bright side of life.

—Sydney Barbara Metrick

acknowledgments

We wish to thank Celestial Arts for recognizing the need for ritual in our culture. We extend our deepest appreciation to Julie Bennett, our editor, for her time, energy, and positive suggestions in improving the second edition of *The Art of Ritual.* Special thanks to Terry Hatcher, whose delightful artwork brings beauty to the pages of this book. And thanks to Angeles Arrien for her work with ritual, and for contributing the foreword.

Renee extends great appreciation to the Holy One for making the process go so smoothly all down the line.

earth page 29

contents

foreword

All cultures recognize the need to ritualize major life transitions. In 1929 anthropologist Arnold van Gennep coined the term *rite of passage* to describe the universal practice of ceremonializing life's major events, including (1) birth—newness; (2) entry—making contact with others; (3) initiation—willingness to learn something new and be tested on it; (4) marriage/mergence—capacity for commitment, integration, and unifying opposites; (5) demonstration—ability to facilitate, heal, teach, guide; (6) attainment—inner contentment, modeling a skill or talent; and (7) death—letting go, moving out from the old into the new.

In his introduction to van Gennep's *The Rites of Passage* (University of Chicago Press, 1960), Solon Kimbala said that it is likely "that one dimension of mental illness may arise because an increasing number of individuals are forced to accomplish their transitions alone and with private symbols." In *The Art of Ritual*, authors Beck and Metrick have created a practical healing manual that provides specific steps and guidelines for rituals. Their book will help individuals and groups learn the art of supporting life changes as well as how to honor the space and time between transitions, an equally important subject largely ignored by this culture. Bill Bridges, in his book *Transitions: Making Sense of Life's Changes* (Perseus Publishing, 1980), calls the area between changes "the neutral zone." The Africans refer to this as "walking the land of gray clouds." We might call this time "the land of I-don't-know."

Our culture has not learned how to support the time between rites of passage or how to honor the need to take the time to incorporate life experiences. During most major life events, for example, a person in this culture is supported strongly for a few weeks or a month, but after that, support problems surface. A person between jobs might be asked, "Well, when are you going to get your next job?" A recently married couple might be asked, "When are you going to have a baby?" Someone experiencing the death of a loved one might be asked, "When are you going to get going again?" The minimum time required by an individual to integrate a consequential life experience is one year, and some people require two years. If one doesn't take time to absorb these experiences when they occur, they can emerge years later and cause other problems, such as untimely depression or unresolved grief. Our lives may be running smoothly, yet a sense of meaninglessness may be present. Such unhappy states indicate the surfacing of unresolved transitions.

One way this culture recognizes the need to ritualize and support change in others is by sending greeting cards. Our society, as it accelerates at a faster rhythm, experiences change at a swifter pace. Greeting cards are quick, efficient messages of support in our rapidly changing world. However, in a slower-moving society in which spending time with an individual or family is a major way of extending support, greeting cards would not be appropriate.

To survive in the twenty-first century, people must become more capable of handling change than ever before. Alvin Toffler elaborates on this idea in his visionary book *Future Shock* (Bantam Books, 1970) when he states, "We have the opportunity to introduce additional stability points and rituals into our society, such as new holidays, pageants, ceremonies, and games. Such mechanisms could not only provide a backdrop of continuity in everyday life but serve to integrate societies, and cushion them somewhat against the fragmenting impact of super-industrialism." Essentially, the challenge in the next century will be to become "the change master," a term Rosabeth Moss Kanter introduced in the 1980s. Kanter identifies ways we cope, manage, resist, or creatively approach change.

The Art of Ritual gives "Ten Guidelines for Creating Your Own Rituals" in Chapter 8: Ritual Guidelines and Worksheet to assist you during times of change. Beck and Metrick also give examples of ways to integrate your experience. They remind us that human beings have used ritual for centuries as an important buffer to change and as a way of consciously recognizing and supporting a life event rather than denying or indulging in it. *The Art of Ritual* provides a structure to recall the truth of Novalis's statement that "the seat of the soul is where the outer and inner worlds meet." Ritual provides the bridge between inner and outer worlds and creates a context for reconnecting to the seat of our souls. The end results of all ritual are increased balance, strength, energy, and comfort. This is an important book whose time has come.

—Angeles Arrien
Cultural Anthropologist

introduction

It is the nature of human beings to grow, to evolve, to increase relationships with ourselves, each other, our world, and with our sense of Spirit. The substance of our lives is based in this process. Connecting with our creative resources, our recognition of wholeness, and more important, with the knowledge that we are part of something much larger that is eternal and omnipresent makes the difference between merely existing and living fully.

Ritual has been a viable access to such a connection throughout human history. The rituals our ancestors used thousands of years ago focused our relationships with the land, the seasons, the hunt, with others in the tribe, and relationships between tribes. Human needs have remained the same, but survival has become more complex. The rituals handed down to us are frequently insufficient to address and satisfy our personal and spiritual needs and often cannot heal us from the separation and alienation so too often experienced in today's world. It is more than apparent that our society and our world are in a frightening and dangerous condition.

The authors have practiced the symbolic and ritual arts for over thirty years and worked as counselors and teachers for over twenty. Through our own inner quests and our intimate work with people dealing with life's challenges, we have come to recognize the need for personalized and meaningful rituals in people's lives. We have created and performed rituals for ourselves, our friends and families, our clients and students. We have learned that creating rituals is not a "one size fits all" process. By being open to differences and possibilities, we have developed and refined the ritual process presented here. We designed this book of ritual guidelines to offer you the means to help yourself, and others, through life's transitions. When you turn to this book to help you create a ritual to dramatize, comment on, and shape an event, you give yourself the opportunity to be "at cause": to be connected with your center, your purpose, your relatedness to other people, our universe, and Spirit. You empower yourself.

A contemporary psychological concept called "locus of control" is a generalized expectancy that one's outcomes are contingent more on one's own efforts than on outside forces such as luck, fate, or the power of others. The former is said to characterize persons with an internal locus of control, whereas the latter characterizes individuals with an external locus of control. When people have an internal locus of control, they feel that by their acts they can have some control and thus some power in their lives.

In *Power and Innocence* (W. W. Norton & Co., 1972), Rollo May states, "Power is the ability to cause or prevent change." He names five kinds of power:

* Exploitative: subjects the weak to the strong with no concern for the needs of the weak.

* Manipulative: power *over* another that requires the collusion, collaboration, and cooperation of the weaker.

* Competitive: power *against* another.

* Nutrient: power used *for* the other to meet the needs of the other.

* Integrative: power used *with* another to build a better life for both.

Synergistics is another way of stating it. Power is made available to the community, and everyone's power is shared.

This book is designed to provide empowerment through nutrient and integrative power. Bringing rituals into your life empowers you. Rituals allow you to have more choices, to gain perspective on changes. Rituals offer you tradition, an increased grasp of relatedness, and a greater sense of balance to help you improve your life. Rituals can help you weather difficulties involved in life transitions.

Transitions are often a form of crisis, an emotionally significant event, or radical change of status in a person's life; an unstable or crucial time. In our secularized, technologically sophisticated society, the existential isolation that all humans experience is exacerbated during a crisis. In our desperate need to find support, connection, or solace, we often focus an exaggerated amount of energy on inappropriate people, substances, or pastimes. A *New York Times* article stated, "These days almost anyone might have an addiction. If it isn't to drugs or alcohol, it's to food, cigarettes, exercise, relationships, sex, shopping, work, or even video games." These "addictions" offer an intimate connection or relationship that, although not fulfilling our real needs, seems to offer some form of appeasement.

Since the September 11, 2001, terrorist acts of aggression against the United States and the war in Iraq, the need for ritual has become increasingly more visible in our culture. The country has begun to realize more deeply the importance of nonmaterial values: family, community, country, and service. Americans have come together as a nation to grieve, with both individuals and communities using ritual as a way to express and transform feelings. We have come to rely on the unifying and healing power of ceremony, and we recognize ritual's ability to make us feel part of a greater whole, of a larger meaning and mission. Through ritual, Americans and other citizens of the world have joined together to express our humanity and commonality.

This need is also reflected in the ways our traditional holidays have become more ritualized, with more people participating in both secular and religious holidays. The ritualization of these events is not always based in religion. It might be more accurate to say they are "spiritually based." People seek balance and harmony. This is reflected in the miniature Zen sand gardens and the small-scale water fountains found in homes and offices and the incorporation of feng shui principles into design to increase peace and prosperity. When people create a ceremony, they transform the environment from the ordinary to the extraordinary with music, language, costume, lighting, and other art forms.

Art and ritual have become expressions of community feeling. Driving through any city, it has become increasingly common to see roadside shrines built to honor loved ones lost to accidents or violence. Over two-thirds of the homes in my neighborhood now decorate for Halloween. Many of these are homes with no children, yet they display hanging pumpkin lights, carved jack-o'-lanterns, cobwebs, scary ghosts and goblins, and even small "graveyards." For Dias del los Muertos (Days of the Dead), festivals and exhibits of *altares* (altars) are common in many neighborhoods. Sugar skulls and other items for *ofrendas* (offerings) are easily found. Halloween and Dias de los Muertos are examples of a growing interest in the spirit world, in bridging the living with their heritage and the legacy of their ancestors.

These rituals are not only a connection with Spirit, they are a way to build fellowship and share the spirit of community.

Our lives have become increasingly busy. The problems we face are of a different kind and scope than we have seen before. Creative thinking and new ways of group brainstorming are necessary to solve our problems. Community has become more important, and we need better ways to network on deeper, more meaningful levels. The art of ritual is a vital part of a greater solution.

Ritual has always been used to honor cultural and personal traditions and turning points; rituals provide a way to reinforce connections among people in the family, the community, or on a spiritual level. When traditional ceremonies no longer hold the sacred, it is necessary for people to expand and deepen existing ritual or create new ones that specifically and clearly address the needs of the time. *The Art of Ritual* guides people in creating new rituals or amending the old to grant us greater access to our personal and community connections, our familial and cultural heritage, and our union with the sacred.

It is our belief that through knowledge and the understanding of ritual we can gain access to timeless wisdom and attain the sense that being is of value in and of itself. To that end, we present the basic elements and processes common to all rituals in an attempt to provide an understanding of how rituals work, as well as the knowledge necessary to create rituals for various occasions. The principles involved are simple but effective. We hope to help you understand the rituals you already use, bring new meaning and depth to ritualized events such as birthdays, New Year's Eve, and housewarmings, and develop new rituals where you might need them in your lives. Beyond this, we hope that the integration of the principles presented here lends a structure to your consciousness that increases the meaning in your day-to-day life. While ritual is a tool to bridge the gap between the sacred and the mundane, we believe that "ordinary" life is sacred, as the expression of Spirit.

how to use this book

We want to share some ideas and techniques that have been a source of support, honor, and assistance through our various life transitions. We have found that using personal rituals has been important in our individual lives, as it has been for our friends, students, and clients. Hopefully, this book will inspire and benefit you.

The chapters in this book form a step-by-step guide to learning and using the concepts fundamental to practicing ritual. Each chapter blends with the others to form a seamless whole. As you read and absorb one chapter, your ability to understand and use the subsequent one will improve. Therefore, we recommend that you read each section before attempting to design your own rituals, even if the ideas in a specific chapter seem intriguing enough to make you want to start right away.

If you are new to the world of ritual, this is especially important. If you are experienced in the practice of ritual, it may still be valuable to familiarize yourself with the particular concepts and processes we discuss, so you can blend your style with the approach we present.

Any ritual you design is an attempt to return to a sense of wholeness that transition has altered. Whether the rite is an effort to correct an imbalance or celebratory of positive change, the growth that results from the planning, preparation, and manifestation should be a reflection of the wholeness contained in the ritual itself.

To this end, we provide self-exploration questions and ideas for projects at the end of each chapter to help you review and integrate the information presented. The exercises focus on helping you to become more conscious of the sacred in your daily life and on familiarizing you with the skills you need to create and perform truly effective rituals. While you may choose to use this book as a reference, use it both as a textbook for creating rituals and as a tool for transformation.

We wrote this book to be an ally in your search for meaning and purpose. The journey into Self requires a commitment. We know some people feel uncomfortable with what this word represents, but the commitment is to deepening your experience of life, connecting with the sacred, and improving yourself, your relationships, and your world. The sign that you are ready to make this commitment is a feeling of excitement about making such a pledge to yourself. To get the most out of your commitment, set aside a minimum of thirty minutes each day for self-work.

This thirty-minute daily practice will become a natural and welcome part of your life. This is a quiet time for you to get to know yourself better and reconnect with your idea of Spirit. After you go through each chapter, working with the self-exploration questions and exercises at the end will help you incorporate the information from that chapter into your life. Daily exercises are provided, as well as different activities. We recommend doing all of them, as they are designed to bring balance among the inspired, thinking, feeling, doing, and healing aspects of the Self. However, depending on your experience, some of the questions may feel too simple or too complicated for you, so feel free to adapt or personalize them so they fit for you. Spending a week or so working on each chapter will bring you skill and insight to use in performing rituals and in designing your life.

Forming a discussion group that meets regularly can also help deepen the work you do, add new perspectives and inspiration, and be a lot of fun. Gather a group of like-minded friends, or connect with others who are interested in the art of ritual. Online discussion is another possibility that lets you connect with a more diverse group, but working together virtually is more of a creative challenge.

The individual work you do will probably be the most rewarding. We suggest getting a special journal to jot down notes as you read *The Art of Ritual* and work the questions at the end of each chapter.

Take your time. As you read through Chapter 1: Understanding the Role of Ritual in Your Life, you may start to recall different rituals that have occurred in your life. Begin to explore how ritual is relevant to changes you have experienced, where you may see the need for ritual, and how ritual can be a powerful, useful tool.

Chapter 2: Myth, History, and Symbol will help you get in touch with the age-old role ritual has played in our lives as humans. You are introduced to the language of symbols and begin to explore how you have used symbols throughout your life as well as how to consciously use them now.

Acquaint yourself with the types of rituals discussed in Chapter 3: Types of Rituals. As you become familiar with the categories, you may begin realizing how different parts of your life fall into one or another grouping. Think about how you currently address or neglect these transitions, and make a mental note regarding those passages in your life in which you might consider introducing ritual.

Chapter 4: The Process of Ritual presents the process for creating and performing a ritual. The concept of process can be difficult for Western minds to accept. Process is not just an approach or method, but a practice. The values of our society orient us toward goals, achievements, and results. The letters *ASAP* form a familiar command: "As Soon As Possible!" Yet the importance of the journey, weighed against arrival at the destination, is interesting to consider. The journey gives the destination worth.

Familiarizing yourself with the developmental stages that unfold during a process and cultivating the careful attention and patience a process requires will help you create rituals with increased power and meaning. Even more important, as you develop the concept of process, your normal life can lose some of the stressful urgency that each of us experiences.

We all have different tools that help us cope. Our techniques vary in their efficacy. When we are in demanding situations, it is not uncommon to rely on some resources past their point of usefulness. You may be a runner, a coffee drinker, or a smoker. Perhaps you bake bread, shoot baskets, or listen to music when you need to come back to yourself. Each of these things works for a reason, as you will see in Chapter 5: The Elements of Ritual, where we introduce you to the Elements. These are capitalized throughout the book to help you recognize them as symbols of archetypal qualities. The information in this section can help you identify the ways you lose your equilibrium during changes. Baking bread may ground you or get you in touch with the Element of Earth. Smoking may seem to clear your head and give you greater access to the Element of Air. By working with the Element Selection Guide, you can bring more resources to your daily life as you learn to choose Elemental symbols for ritual harmony.

Finding a way to make these symbols tangible turns them from concepts to useful tools. In Chapter 6: Crafting and Consecrating Tools, find simple instructions for making tools that serve as power objects. Bringing these power objects into your rituals is one way a ceremony becomes a sacred rite. The way you use your tools as part of the ritual creates another opportunity to transform the energy of the ceremony into a moving and magical experience.

Chapter 7: Altars contains information on setting up altars. An altar is a kind of mirror with each of the Elements symbolically represented in the balanced way you hope to become within yourself. As you arrange your altar, reflect on the connection with your inner state.

Basic principles are involved in the design and use of altars. As you become familiar with the principles, you will recognize the expression of the sacred in even the simplest altar. An altar is a place from which you work, the place that holds your ritual tools and power objects. Setting up an altar that holds these objects in a sacred and balanced way is the first step toward creating the same balance within.

When you reach Chapter 8: Ritual Guidelines and Worksheet, you will be comfortable with all of the aspects and details of creating a successful ritual. Here the step-by-step worksheet will help you plan each stage of the rituals you create.

In Chapter 9: Applications of Ritual, find a number of actual ceremonies that have been designed to describe each of the ritual types we categorize: beginnings, mergings, cycles, endings, and healings. We subcategorize these samples in two specific ways. In each of the five categories, there is a sample designed for individual use, one for two individuals in a relationship, one for a family, and one for a group. In each of those subcategories, find a ritual example for the physical world of manifestation, the feeling world of deepening, the mental world of relatedness, and the spiritual world of initiation. Some of the rituals described will be directly useful, and if not, adaptable to your needs.

Chapter 10 is the conclusion to *The Art of Ritual,* and the self-exploration questions should help you integrate what you learn from the book and your work with it, as well as focus you on the role of ritual in your life in the future.

In the appendixes, we present two complete rituals that follow each step as shown in Chapter 4: The Process of Ritual. Here you can find insight and ideas to bring to your own rituals. Appendix A also contains a table of Elemental correspondences to help you in your ritual planning.

There is an art to the creation of a successful ritual. Each ceremony is a dramatic event that opens the door to another world. Entering this world is similar to what you might experience during a movie, play, concert, or religious service. You can become so absorbed in the experience that the feelings evoked remove you from where, and even who, you are. The world you enter through ritual is a timeless one. It lies within you, in a place often unremembered, and around you, in a place often beyond reach.

The Art of Ritual is designed to show you ways to create access to that inner world, to help you connect with Spirit, with the wisdom of our collective human consciousness, and a sense of meaning and purpose. Ritual can help empower you in making decisions, expanding community, and weathering difficult and painful transitions. It can help you better celebrate the joys in human existence and bring beauty and a sense of wonder back into your life. At its best, ritual is a truly transformative experience, and the knowledge to create such powerful tools lies in the pages ahead.

CHAPTER 1

understanding the role of ritual in your life

A ritual, a rite, a ceremony, a series of symbolic acts focused toward fulfilling a particular intention. We often think of ritual as belonging to the realm of religion, but in fact, rituals are an integral part of nature and our daily lives. Animals have ritualized ways of defining and defending their territory, and humans do as well. Animals and birds often have elaborate courting and mating rituals, again, not unlike humans. Finding, collecting, preparing, and eating food is another behavior that is ritualized for us as it is in nature. When we look at survival or social behavior, we generally see ritual.

In this book, we intend to focus not on the unconscious rituals that give form to life, but on the ones that we consciously create with intentionality. Many unconscious rituals exist in our daily lives: the morning coffee and newspaper, tucking the children into bed with a story, playing softball with our friends every week, or sleeping in on Sunday mornings. Other rituals that have a place in our lives, that have a more conscious intent and sense of magic, fall into the category of holidays. These are occasions such as birthdays, weddings, winter celebrations, graduation ceremonies, and baby showers. Certainly the celebration of these events offers a sense of enhanced meaning, an opportunity for increased social connection, and a deepening of tradition. What the *traditional rituals* may not provide is something that speaks to your individual needs in a profound and meaningful manner.

THE PURPOSE OF RITUAL

Transitions or turning points, even when positive, signify moving toward something new and possibly unfamiliar. What was may be incorporated and used as a springboard toward the new, or we may leave it behind. Those aspects of change—the unknown ahead and the loss of what was—can make the experience of change difficult. We often undergo a period of feeling out of balance until we can accustom ourselves to the differences. Even when the life change is a sought-after improvement such as a new job, it is not uncommon to find that the first weeks bring the confusion and insecurity of adjusting to a new role, new coworkers in a new environment, and new responsibilities. These adjustments can supersede the pride and elation that initially accompanied the job move. Discovering ways to incorporate and adjust to the newness can be a demanding challenge. It entails finding an equilibrium between the outer expression of the change and our inner relationship to it. Possible ways of accomplishing this at the new workplace may include improving and deepening communication with coworkers, clearly defining job responsibilities, and getting support from friends and family during this time of adjustment. When this inner-outer balance occurs, we may realize a calming sense of wholeness.

On a transpersonal level, this wholeness is really never lost, but on a personal level, we can easily lose touch with it. In *The Power of Myth*, Bill Moyers, in conversation with Joseph Campbell, says, "The wise people of all times have said that we can live the good life if we learn to live spiritually.... How do we learn to live spiritually?" And Campbell replies, "In ancient times...that was what ritual was for. A ritual can be defined as an *enactment* of a myth. By participating in a ritual, you are actually experiencing a mythological life. And it's out of that participation that one can learn to live spiritually" (Doubleday, 1988).

This is the purpose of creative ritual—increasing balance and connection in ourselves, with one another, the world, and with the larger rhythms and energies that bring stability and light to our lives. Many of the rituals available to us may seem empty. Our needs, as individuals and as a people, have changed. The traditional rituals may not meet or even recognize our current needs. When rituals are so finely woven into the fabric of our common expressions that we barely recognize them for what they are, much less tap into their inherent power, it is time to take a look at how we can once again actively bring ritual to a meaningful and relevant position. This requires first taking an honest look at our lives and the trends and values of our culture.

Once we are in touch with our identity we can create rituals appropriate to our needs. Our personal and cultural myths may unconsciously guide us, but offer little emotional support unless we can consciously express what they symbolize. Joseph Campbell, in *Myths to Live By* (Bantam Books, 1972), sees mythology as having four functions.

* Mystical or metaphysical: Its purpose is to bring the individual to a state of wonder at the mystery of it all—from the universal level to the personal level.

* Cosmological: The function here is to bring the mystery, expressed in universal themes and motifs, to the people of each culture in a way that helps them understand their world.

* Sociological: It provides a way of verifying, nurturing, and preserving the beliefs and customs of a culture or social order.

* Psychological: Myth is a guide and a support to individuals from birth to death and through the difficult passages of human life. As we develop the ability to step back from life and see the stories we tell

"People…create images of themselves in the world and guide their action according to such images. The images are not only myths that capture the meaning of past experiences but lead to anticipation of future events."

—N. Fredman and R. Sherwood, *Handbook of Structured Techniques in Marriage and Family Therapy* both individually and in the various groups to which we belong, we will then look at our myths; we can then use ritual to enact them in a way that empowers us.

THE RELEVANCE OF RITUAL

To derive power from a ritual it must, in some way, stand apart from our ordinary lives. It is not uncommon for so much of our energy and attention to be directed toward our daily routines and our goals that our focus becomes narrowed. We may even become preoccupied with our doubts, our fears, or our pain. These things can isolate us. We may lose connection with the rhythm in our lives and the passages we all share as human beings on the planet. This is what the existential philosopher Martin Heidegger called a state of "forgetfulness of being."

On the other hand, there is the state of "mindfulness of being." This is a condition of authenticity, of being fully self-aware and conscious of being the creative composer of one's own life. Ritual provides us with a way of taking responsibility for our lives through the use of a metaphoric process. At the time of a milestone or rite of passage, we can shift our focus from the minutiae of the event to the way the experience fits into the grand plan of life. The creativity, drama, and perceptual shift connected with the ritual enable us to disidentify with the isolation, confusion, or fear associated with the passage and to know instead the power of creativity, action, and understanding.

Ritual is often recognized as an art form. The ceremoniously performed acts of a ritual allow us to form a connection with the unconscious as we begin to speak its language. Not only can we access our individual unconscious, which holds that which has passed from awareness, but we summon energy from the collective unconscious as well. Here we pass through our roots into our ancestral heritage, which is common to the human family. This essential energy is expressed as mythological motifs that transcend history and cultural differences and establishes instead a fundamental sense of unity.

THE POWER OF RITUAL

A well-designed and executed ritual is more than just a dramatic presentation. Through ritual we can enter a state of timelessness, which is sometimes called an altered state of consciousness. In this state, we can go beyond the parameters that describe our perception of reality. The transformative power of a ritual comes by way of this altered state, which Milton Erickson, M.D., known as the world's leading practitioner of medical hypnosis during his lifetime, describes as a trance state:

> *This healing or therapeutic condition of trance "is a period during which the limitations of one's usual frames of reference and beliefs are temporarily altered so one can be receptive to other patterns of association and modes of mental functioning that are conducive to problem solving."*

In *An Explanatory Casebook* (Irvington Publishers, 1979), Erickson develops a five-step paradigm for achieving therapeutic trance, which is parallel to what occurs in achieving any altered state. The steps are as follows:

1. Fixation of attention, anything that fascinates and holds or absorbs a person's attention;

2. Habitual...beliefs are more or less interrupted and suspended for a moment or two...;

3. Unconscious search; and

"Directed energy causes change. To have integrity, we must recognize that our choices bring about consequences, and that we cannot escape responsibility for the consequences, not because they are imposed by some external authority, but because they are inherent in the choices themselves."

—Starhawk,
Dreaming the Dark

4. Unconscious process, where a new experience or solution to a problem is sought and a creative moment can occur; and

5. Hypnotic response, an expression of behavioral potentials.

This timeless state, coupled with the expressive, moving, and even spectacular qualities of a dramatic ceremony, brings us to a grander level of experience—a level at which we can feel our own majesty.

When we use ritual to assist us through change, we gain authority not only from the enactment of the ritual, but also from the intentional planning process. When the transition that initially brings the call for support is a difficult passage, it is not uncommon to feel diminished by the power of the change. With the loss of a spouse, we not only have to deal with mourning our loss, but we must also look ahead to a drastically different future. Even when change is something we seek, it is not always easy to accept. A teenager graduating from high school may feel proud of the accomplishment and excited to be free from the school system, but terrified about entering the "adult" world of work or higher education. Entering into a new situation means entering into something unfamiliar, into an arena in which we have less control simply because of the unfamiliarity.

A resistance to change exists in the psychological world as well as the world of physics. Newton's first law states that an object persists in its state of rest or uniform motion unless it is *compelled* to change. Unfortunately, or fortunately, we are often compelled to change. As long as we feel we have some sort of control over what is happening, we do not feel stripped of power. As we plan and prepare for the ritual event, we are involved in the process of *doing* versus *being done to*. This in itself is empowering.

We are all familiar with the difference in feeling between the empowerment of action and the powerlessness that can follow being acted upon. This is apparent even in the informal rituals we enact to gain a sense of control over our lives. These are actions such as fighting an unfair parking violation and leaving the courtroom fine-free and gratified. Although in a case such as this we are still at the mercy of the machinations of "the system," we find there is opportunity, through our own creative response, to be more than a powerless victim. The same creativity that brings this option is the foundation of ritual expression. And the kind of power to which one is restored through the use of ritual is nothing less than a return to our own spiritual center, the home of our self-esteem.

THE NEED FOR RITUAL

As Western civilization has advanced, secularization has increased and the connection to the sacred has declined. The individualism nourished by the "me generation" in the sixties opened us up to more acceptance of differences. Yet the diversity born from fearlessly seeking our differences distanced us from the spiritual containers previously provided by simple reliance on family, neighborhood, or church. We often found ourselves left on our own to deal with the changes in our lives. Solon Kimbala, in his introduction to Arnold van Gennep's *The Rites of Passage* (University of Chicago Press, 1960), writes that it is likely "that one dimension of mental illness may arise because an increasing number of individuals are forced to accomplish their transitions alone and with

"Any affect or emotion which in its raw and unaltered form is too intense to be controlled by will alone may need its ritual. Without ritual, such energies may inundate the ego and force it into acting out or into obsessive behavior. Ritual brings about containment and acceptance, control of intensity, and 'dosage.'"

—Edward Whitmont,
Return of the Goddess

private symbols." As individuals, we need more relatedness and better ways to find a balance in ourselves.

Socially, we need to create more balance as well. There is no denying that as a people and as a planet, we need healing. Unless we find ways to achieve harmony in ourselves and in our relationships with others, and learn to consciously unite as members of a global family, the dangers we face will continue to increase. Mystical traditions propose that the one goal of personal growth is to become more conscious of all our relationships, inner and outer, and with our sense of Spirit, until we recognize it as a sense of unity or oneness among all things. Even if we are not spiritually inclined, the need for an increased awareness and balanced unification seems evident if we are to succeed in avoiding destruction of our species and our planet.

Ritual is one way to help this process of growth. People not presently involved with a traditional religion deserve access to safe and life-affirming ritual methods with which they can feel comfortable. Those in religious or spiritual traditions can benefit by a more conscious understanding of the rituals they utilize. Both can benefit by bringing awareness and intention to the secular rituals that are a regular part of life.

Our intention with this book is to help you understand the meaning of ritual and to teach you how ritual can enhance your life. Even more, we wish to give you tools to use to support your life transitions. As explained in the Introduction, we add journaling exercises at the end of each chapter to help you better understand and integrate the information presented in each chapter.

SELF EXPLORATION

Answering the following questions will help you gain a greater understanding of any life transition by way of exploring how the purpose, relevance, and power of ritual may apply. Use your journal to note your thoughts and feelings.

1. Purpose. Identify a transition you are undergoing. It can be connected with career, relationship, or another aspect of your life.

   Note how this change affects the balance in your life: what is becoming more important and less important?

   To incorporate this change into your life in a positive way:

   What do you need to do or have?

   What feelings do you need to address?

   What new information do you need?

   How do you need to be different?

2. Relevance. How do you want this transition to impact who and how you are in your life now and in the future? How is this change relevant to the "big picture" of who you are?

   How do you connect with the "big picture"? Think of the times you felt connected with the universe, at peace, or filled with love and wonder—if only for a moment. Music, personal connection, nature, or beauty sometimes gives rise to these feelings. Write about these experiences. Include your feelings, thoughts, sensations, and energy. How did these experiences affect your life, your perceptions, or beliefs?

3. Power. Connecting with the universal aspect of Self reminds you that at your center you are constant and balanced; when you undergo transition, your outer self, and your idea of yourself, changes. It is especially important during change to be able to access balance. We all have different things we do that help us feel centered; exercise, meditation, breathing, and being in nature are a few. Make a list of all the things you can think of that help bring you back to yourself.

Commit to using one or more of these tools every day, and record your experiences in your journal. Make a note of which tool you are going to use.

4. Need. How can this transition help you increase relationship? With yourself? friends? family? coworkers? community? school? political action? spirit? service? Choose one way you want this change to increase your relatedness.

How can you start improving that relationship now?

At the end of the week, read over your journal entries. Write down what you learned and anything new you notice from reading through your experiences this week.

CHAPTER 2

myth, history, and symbol

The use of ritual is parallel with the emergence of humankind. Two to three million years ago, humans depended primarily on the hunt, and they created the first rituals to appease nature and ensure survival. They made sacrifices to the hunted animals to guarantee that the tribes' needs for food would be met. These animals, such as the cave bear and the cave lion, were also seen to have a religious power and significance that led them to be used as totems. Such totems were used chiefly for protection, but were also seen as ways to provide an alliance with the animal pack.

MYTH AND HISTORY

Evidence exists that 150,000 years ago *Homo sapiens neanderthalensis*—the Neanderthal—dealt with the mystery of life by the ritual burial of their dead. Remains have been unearthed in Europe that held tools, weapons, and other objects that point to a belief in some sort of after-life. Shrines were also found with altars to the animals slain during hunts. These Paleolithic people are known for elaborate paintings depicting the hunt and the part the sorcerer or shaman played in it. The wondrous paintings of these hunters have been found in labyrinthine caves in France and also in North Africa.

According to Joseph Campbell in *Primitive Mythology* (Penguin Books, 1987), the totemistic hunters described above belonged to one of three basic types of primitive societies distinguished by Father W. Schmidt in *The Origin of the Idea of God.*

> *These groups, with secret initiation rites, elaborate clan systems, and tribal traditions emphasized the role and authority of men, both in the religious and the political organization of the symbolically articulated community. Another type of peoples were involved with hunting, fishing, and gathering. An essential equality existed between the sexes, with different tasks not promoting any special privileges or peculiar rights to command. A third type of people with a social organization almost completely antithetical to that of the hunting tribes could be found in the tropical gardening cultures. Here women enjoyed the magico-religious and social advantage. They were the bearers of children and chief producers of food.*

The women of the Stone Age, in addition to being depicted in the many cave paintings, are also represented by carved female figures, often known as Venus figures. The small nude figures, with exaggerated breasts, bellies, and hips, are believed to embody the concept of fertility. Representing the archetypal female, they symbolize both the mystery of life and birth in women, as expressed by "Mother Earth." The people of the Stone Age were nature worshipers: the sunrise heralding the day, the sunset bringing on the night, the phases of the moon, and the passing of seasons were all mysteries that profoundly influenced their lives. Rituals were created to ensure the rising of the sun, the falling of the rain, and the fertility of the earth. We find the roots of many of our present celebrations in the rituals and holidays developed by these nature-worshiping peoples.

According to Clifford Geertz in *Magic, Witchcraft, and Religion* (Mayfield Publishing, 1985), the primitive people of these early tribes used symbol and ritual in an instinctive way.

> *Magic was the primordial form of human thought; it consisted in either spatiotemporal connection ("sympathetic magic," as when drinking the blood of an ox transfers its strength to the drinker) or phenomenal similarity ("imitative magic," as when the sound of drumming induces thunderheads to form).*

In a symbolic manner, a level of reality was ritually created that became the consensual reality of daily life.

Ancient history shows that the participation mystique of the earliest peoples was the directing force that created the numinous quality of their symbolic and real lives. This same quality of merging the subjective and objective belongs to all of us in our early years of childhood. The development of consciousness, in the individual as in the race, shifts the ways symbol and ritual are used; but perhaps the innate quality of magical thinking is what allows symbol, ritual, myth, and religion to manifest in our lives.

SYMBOLS AND THE COLLECTIVE UNCONSCIOUS

Symbols have a level of universal meaning and a level of personal meaning. Symbols are the language of the unconscious mind, and according to Jungian psychology, a personal unconscious (those memories from one's own history that are not immediately or easily available) exists as well as a collective unconscious. In *Boundaries of the Soul* (Anchor Press, 1973), June Singer states:

> The collective unconscious may be thought of as an impersonal or transpersonal unconscious because as Jung says, "It is detached from anything personal and is entirely universal, and because its contents can be found everywhere, which is naturally not the case with personal contents." The collective unconscious is better conceived as an extension of the personal unconscious to its wider and broader base, encompassing contents which are held in common by the family, by the social group, by tribe and nation, by race, and eventually by all humanity. Each succeeding level of the unconscious may be thought of as going deeper and becoming more collective in its nature. The wonder of the collective unconscious is that it's all there, all the legend and history of the human race, with its unexorcised demons and its gentle saints, its mysteries and its wisdom, all within each one of us—a microcosm within the macrocosm.

We can gain a better understanding of how symbols express the archetypal energies of the collective unconscious by exploring one of these archetypes. The archetypal feminine, exemplified by the earth mother figures described earlier, is one of these energies. This psychic phenomenon has been symbolically and ritually expressed from the magical phase of Paleolithic consciousness, through the mythological phase of Neolithic consciousness, into the Bronze and Iron Ages and beyond. We find this energy in the myths, rituals, and symbols of all times and cultures. In early times, the earth mother was known as the Mother Goddess or the Great Goddess. The Goddess energy represented not only creation and fertility, but also death and a subsequent rebirth that began the cycle anew. This and other archetypal energies find their way into mythological motifs that support the universal nature of the collective unconscious. The death-rebirth cycle associated with the Great Goddess is itself an archetypal expression. The cycle of the opposites embraced in a whole, the dynamic interplay between these polar forces, and even more primarily, the undifferentiated state that precedes bifurcation are recognized in other cultures with different symbols.

This cycle of continuity, also known as the Great Round, was symbolically depicted as the Ouroboros—the snake biting its own tail. The image of a snake is universally recognized as a powerful symbol. The meanings include transformation (the snake shedding its skin and being regenerated), creativity (the dynamic expansion represented by its phallic shape), temptation (the seduction of strength by matter), and inner strength (as in the yoga concept of kun-

"Diel rightly asserts that the
symbol is a vehicle at once
universal and particular.
Universal, since it transcends
history; particular, because it
relates to a definite period of
history."

—J. E. Cirlot,
A Dictionary of Symbols

dalini energy). On the collective level, the meanings for the snake are many and often paradoxical. On a personal level, the associations one has with snakes may come from other sources. This could be the subjective interpretation one makes of the snake story in Genesis. Associations may come from a highly charged experience in one's personal history—having a family member with a snake phobia, for example. The connections that we can evoke are limitless.

THE FUNCTION OF SYMBOLS

A symbol is something that represents something else. The role of symbols in ritual is largely as vehicles through which one can join forces with the essential concordance of the group, nature, the universe, or Spirit. Through the language of the unconscious, we address the deeper levels of our individual and collective selves when we use symbols. Paul Tillich, in *Theology and Symbolism* (F. Ernest Johnson, 1955), wrote that this is the great function of symbols: to point beyond themselves with a power greater than the symbols themselves, "to open up levels of reality which otherwise are closed, and to open up levels of the human mind of which we otherwise are not aware." In studying mythology, folklore, or comparative religion, it soon becomes evident that many symbols and themes are repeated, sometimes only slightly altered, from culture to culture over time. The Christian sacrament of communion, or "eating the god" to make him a part of you, has parallels in many other traditions. In agrarian cultures, a ceremony is performed at every harvest to insure the crop's abundance in the following year. This entails making bread with the last sheaves of corn and ritually consuming it. The ceremony is based on the belief that the "corn god" that lives in the crops remains immortal as his life is transmuted. We find similar rituals in the traditions of pre-Columbian Aztecs, North American Creek Indians, and other peoples from India to Africa to Japan.

When one performs the symbolic act of eating (taking in, becoming one with, being nourished by) the fruit or bread that represents God or Spirit, the opportunity is afforded to experience something that one could not otherwise experience. The symbol and the symbolic act that imply something greater provide the means to know or to be something greater than oneself—to move from the secular toward the sacred.

SYMBOLS

Some symbols have a solely personal meaning. Symbolic objects in your life may hold meaning only for you. The back corner of your closet may hold a cherished pair of tattered old sneakers that you just can't throw away. You wore them when you scored the winning points in a basketball game. If anyone saw them, they might think the pride associated with that occasion is the reason for your attachment to the sneakers. But for you, they may symbolize something even greater—a turning point in your life. Others may not be aware of the insecurities you conquered to play in that game or that you had to let go of the thought of possible humiliation to put every ounce of courage and effort into that critical shot—and you did it! Since that day, you have walked in a different world, one in which you are more confident and courageous. The sneakers became a personal symbol of transformation for you.

Other symbols, although personal, may be shared. These are found frequently in relationships and families. One of our clients shared a family story that exemplifies this. When Cindy was seven, her mother, who loathed sewing, hand stitched a family flag. She sewed a maroon symbol representing each family member onto a turquoise field. The household was quite proud of this flag and flew it in front of their home on family occasions and holidays. The flag became a symbol of unity for the family. Years later, after all the children had grown, left home, and started their own families, Cindy was one day honored by the gift of this flag. It became a treasured keepsake for her.

Mementos too, or souvenirs, often serve as symbols, not only to remind people of an experience they had, but also to bring forth the feelings associated with that time.

Just as families may have symbols that bring them a sense of unity, so do social groups, organizations, and even nations. These symbols bring a sense of tradition that binds the group in certain ways. The symbols may say something about the social relationships in the group, such as with uniforms and insignia, or they may express opinions and values common to the group. A logo including a dove or an olive branch, which are symbols for peace, is an example of this. Folklore and cultural myths are made of the symbols and motifs that prescribe the rituals of the group. As Joseph Campbell stated in *The Power of Myth* (Doubleday, 1988):

> *These bits of information from ancient times, which have to do with the themes that have supported human life, built civilizations, and informed religions over millennia, have to do with deep inner problems, inner mysteries, inner thresholds of passage.... Once this subject catches you, there is such a feeling, from one or another of these traditions, of information of a deep, rich, life-vivifying sort that you don't want to give up.*

In *Folklore, Mythology, and Legend* (Harper and Row, 1984), Funk and Wagnall elaborate on this:

> The "group characteristics" which result from the accumulated nature of folklore [or myth, or ritual], and by which we attempt to recognize and label it, are not to be thought of as opposed to individuality. Folklore is something which the individual has in common with his fellows, just as all have eyes and hands and speech. It is not contrary to himself as an individual but a part of his equipment. It makes possible—perhaps it might be defined as that which constitutes—his rapport with his particular segment of mankind.

When you determine the symbols to use in a ritual, you not only choose things and acts that have a personal meaning for you, but perhaps unknown to you, the choices you make likely tap into a greater and more profound history that is accessible through your own unconscious. When you think of history, you generally think in a linear fashion of history being behind you. By considering history as being created cyclically, season after season, year after year, it may be easier to imagine it as the core somewhere within the unconscious.

SACRED SYMBOLS

Symbols are an approach to the sacred as they represent common ideas and feelings from the whole of human existence and fundamental concepts about all of existence. Mircea Eliade, in *The Two and the One* (University of Chicago Press, 1962), states:

"Symbolism is organized in its vast, explanatory and creative function as a system of highly complex relations, one in which the dominant factor is always a polarity linking the physical and metaphysical worlds."

—J. E. Cirlot,
A Dictionary of Symbols

The man who understands a symbol not only "opens him-self" to the objective world, but at the same time succeeds in emerging from his personal situation and reaching a comprehension of the universal.... Thanks to the symbol, the individual experience is "awoken" and translated into a spiritual act. To "live" a symbol and correctly decipher its message implies an opening towards the Spirit and finally access to the universal.

Symbols and ritual put us in touch with meaning and mystery in a way nothing else can. In *The Search for Signs of Intelligent Life in the Universe,* Trudy the Bag Lady (played by Lily Tomlin) ponders the meaning of life and says, "The mystery of life. The operative word here is what? Mystery! Not meaning.... Because at the moment you are most in awe of all there is about life that you don't understand, you are closer to understanding it all than at any other time." The power that instills in us wonder and fear, although often incomprehensible or at least ineffable, is still compelling. We constantly seek to move beyond ourselves through music, art, dance, drama, nature, and love, as well as through participation in religious or spiritual activities. From teenagers at a rock concert to families gathered to hear Handel's *Messiah* at Christmas, the common experience produced by the music as well as the event is to be touched and expanded, to be able to turn to someone near us and see that the same feelings were evoked in them, and to feel that unity.

The power of these symbols not only moves us, but also instructs us. Sacred symbols, as the components of mythologies, form the underpinnings of each culture. In every culture, the archetypes (basic energy patterns in the psyche) are represented in this way. Consider, for example, the gods and goddesses of ancient Rome: Juno, the jealous wife; Venus, goddess of love and beauty; Mars, the aggressive god of war; or Pluto, lord of Hades, domain of death and riches. These and many others were worshiped as deities, and at the same time, they derived their power from the fact that they were reflections of the parts in each of us. Their battles are our battles, and their wisdom, ours as well.

SELF EXPLORATION

Reflect on the following questions to better understand the symbols that are part of your life. Note your thoughts and feelings in your journal.

1. Personal Symbols. Different symbols hold differing energies and possibly different meanings for us during our lives. Think about the main symbols that have been active in your personal history. Write or draw the symbols, what they meant to you, and how you used them.

2. The Function of Symbols and Understanding Symbols. Which of these symbols still have meaning for you? Is the meaning the same or different?

   Is there a way you can use this symbol or symbols as you address your current transition?

   What other symbols can you use to help you now?

3. Sacred Symbols. What makes a symbol sacred for you?

   Is there a sacred symbol that will help you in your present transition?

   What does it signify to you?

   How can it be of assistance?

At the end of the week, read over your journal entries. Write down what you learned and anything new you notice from reading through your experiences this week.

CHAPTER 3

types of rituals

All rituals center around transition—changes that have happened, are happening, or may happen. We can divide these changes into five categories—beginnings, mergings, cycles, endings, and healings. Each of these touches on the archetypes you will find repeated a number of times in this book and explained in detail in Chapter 5: The Elements of Ritual. These are the following:

* Initiation or origin (the Element Fire)

* Relatedness (Air)

* Movement or deepening (Water)

* Manifestation or completion (Earth)

* Wholeness or unity (Essence)

Each category has its own integrity but simultaneously entails elements of some or all of the other categories. For example, marriage is a typical example of the merging rituals. Although the main theme of marriage is the coming together of two people to create a shared life, no less important is the ending of single life. This ending is casually addressed in rituals such as bachelor parties. The newly married couple may begin life in a new dwelling, incorporating the category of beginnings. Marriage also necessitates the harmonizing of two individuals with different backgrounds, habits, and ways of being. Sometimes working out these differences requires that the couple enter therapy for each to resolve old individual wounds. Either of these would be a type of healing ritual. The merging, which results in a union greater than the two individuals, may itself provide access to healing. As the years pass and the couple grows together, they celebrate anniversaries, which are cyclical rituals.

Thus, what seems like one event can include the five facets covered by the ritual categories: beginnings, mergings, cycles, endings, and healings. We introduce you to the five categories, give you a few sample rituals, and begin to acquaint you with the suggested format for creating rituals, which is discussed in greater detail in Chapter 4: The Process of Ritual.

BEGINNINGS

"It's a girl!" states the banner across the front window of the corner shop. "Eight pounds, three ounces. Born June 21," it reads. Inside the shop everyone is smiling, and the new father hands cigars to anyone who enters as he shows Polaroid shots of a bald, patchy baby who, in his eyes, is obviously the most beautiful creature on the planet.

Birth is one of the most joyous beginnings, and one that we usually celebrate. Whenever birth occurs—an artist giving creative birth to a painting, symphony, or play; a writer giving birth to a book; a cook giving birth to a souffle; or a cat bearing a litter of tiny, mewing kittens—there is a sense of accomplishment and pride. Celebration is certainly appropriate. We experience many beginnings in our lives, some that are celebrated and honored, some that could be but are not.

There are new jobs, new homes—especially the first apartment or home of one's own—getting accepted to college, or being elected to a particular position. All are worthy of celebration; all are important transitions. We could also recognize puberty, menses, first teeth, first steps, entering adulthood, first gray hair, and the like as beginnings of stages, as markings of time. Whether these beginnings are joyous or difficult, whether they are a cause for rejoicing or for concern, a ritual can give them greater value.

One of the effects of ritual is to deepen our experience, to help us touch on the mythic world, and in rituals honoring beginnings, we reenact the beginning of the universe, the sowing of the seeds of existence. In comparison with this archetypal origination, getting one's first job or reaching puberty may seem inconsequential, but in our unconscious, we relive this archetypal myth of creation with each new beginning; this can sometimes be seen in the accompanying fear and trembling that are more appropriate to the dawn of time than to getting one's driver's license.

While the conscious experience of such changes may be limited to what we think about and sometimes feel, we live our lives on many other levels as well. We may only hear echoes of these deeper movements in our daily ploddings, or glance into them through potent dreams, but they are real. Ritual serves to honor not only our outward changes, but the inner, mythic motions of our souls as well.

One soul-shaking initiation we all experience is puberty. In other cultures, the entry into social sexuality/adulthood is often met with elaborate rites of passage. Puberty is an awkward and difficult time. It marks the beginning of one of the longest and rockiest transitions we may ever experience. Approximately seven arduous years exist between childhood and young adulthood. These years are marked by radical and uncontrollable bodily changes; fierce, rapidly changing emotional states; an entirely new way of thinking; and an almost constant identity crisis. The teenager has one foot in the world of the child and one foot in the world of the adult, and the chasm between the worlds widens unbearably. What could possibly allay the difficulty of this excruciating roller coaster ride? Let us not suggest that a ritual could magically solve a seven-year crisis, but let's look realistically at what is needed to make this transition easier. Often this progression is made more difficult by family members who did not receive the help they needed at this turning point in their lives and who may be experiencing their own confusion about this changing child and the reverberating family impact.

Whenever a family member goes through a major shift, so does the family. This can raise a lot of fear. Everyone needs to recognize that the adolescent's role in the family is changing. Childhood is slowly and gradually being left behind. The teenager may at times want to fully assume the adult role with all its privileges, yet as a child, still fears the responsibilities. It is important to support the emerging identity, however it may choose to manifest. The following is an example of a beginning ritual that could help in this transition.

RITUAL ADDRESSED TO A TEENAGER
This ritual can help the transition from childhood to a new phase of life: adolescence.

Intention: To put behind the old in a safe and gentle way and to consider and prepare for the new.

Preparation: Perhaps you, the teenager, can arrange to spend time in your room with three large boxes, one for that which you have outgrown and no longer need (certain toys, games, books, or mementos), one for those things you have outgrown but with emotional value (a teddy bear or a jersey from a winning Little League game), and one for the things that are currently relevant to your life (particular records or books, jewelry, favorite art). Think about what it would mean to give away childish items to another, younger child. These would be the things in box one. Think about what it means to not want to give up certain items associated with childhood and having that be okay. These are the things to put in box two. Think about how the things for box three symbolize how you see yourself now. As you put objects in their appropriate boxes—which you may decorate in ways that represent how you feel about yourself at these different stages of your life—you may find yourself feeling sadness, pride, anger, fear, or joy. Let these feelings happen; perhaps write about your experience in a journal. Have someone you trust with you if the feelings seem too much to handle alone. Every transition brings up emotions, often conflicting ones. Working them through is an important part of your change, of your sense of who you are, and of who you are becoming.

To help develop this sense of who you can be, plan to add items to box three that represent what might be important to how you would like to see yourself and have others see you. Ask your family members to think about something you might like and/or need to help you in

"Myth not only teaches and regulates, it heals and transforms. To enter into the mythical dimension is to enter into the time of primordial unity, a time when all things were and are in order. If there is a substance or aspect in man needful of redemption, healing and transformation, then contact with this other reality rejuvenates that part. The passion we refer to in talking of the need for mythical ritual arises when the two dimensions—the transpersonal and the mundane—are brought into contact with one another through the mediating act of the ritual. It is the spark which flies when the two stones are struck together, the mysterium tremendum accompanying every truly religious experience, and the cure for spiritual sterility."

—Charles Ponce,
Kabbalah

your growth. It might be a tangible gift such as a razor or a thesaurus, or something such as guitar lessons or a certificate for a week with a half-hour extended curfew.

Manifestation: Invite your family to meet in your room at a designated time. Clean and arrange the room in a way that reflects your identity. Greet your family members and seat them around the room. Talk with them—as much as you feel comfortable—about what is in each of the three boxes and about your process in putting the boxes together. Particular focus should be on the third, the "present and future" box. The family should listen intently and try to discover how willing they are to support your choices. As you present the contents of the third box, each family member should be prepared to offer a gift in harmony with your needs, which may also benefit you in who you feel you are becoming as you grow toward adulthood. A gift honoring a precious part of yourself of which you may be unaware, but that others may recognize and nourish, would also be appropriate. Then form a circle, in which everyone holds hands and pledges to honor each other's struggles and growth and offers to help make this time as easy as possible. After the circle, there can be a sharing of food or drink, made more relevant if you prepared it.

Grounding: You should designate a time to give away the things in the first box to a younger child who would benefit from them. It would be useful to check the things in the second box on a monthly basis to see how much energy they still hold and what you can pass on to someone else. It is important for the family to honor the use of the things in the third box and for all family members to remember and honor their pledge. To help you in each of these grounding steps, you may find writing in your journal helpful, as well as speaking to your family about some of the changes you feel happening in you. Thanking them for their gifts, and letting them know how using them helps you in your transition, can keep you in touch with your process and also honors an adult mode of communication in your new life.

Like all beginning rituals, this one represents an initiation of the Self, a movement toward individuation that is yours alone, through which you must pass alone. For that reason, the support of and connection with others is truly important to help you with your solitary struggles and movements. Your efforts may remind you and those around you of the beginning of something even larger than adolescence. You are in fact recreating in your life the labor and birthing of existence, the mythic emergence of something out of nothing, and the dawning of a new consciousness.

MERGINGS

Initiations, even when honored with the presence of others, are always solitary transitions. Mergings are also beginnings, but they recognize that we do not have to do some things alone. There are, in fact, some things we cannot do alone. When an individual develops sufficiently to recognize distinctions between oneself and others, to realize one's own uniqueness and the uniqueness of others, then relatedness becomes possible and desirable.

In cyclical celebrations, we may join with others to commemorate certain rhythms in our lives and often in the lives of all humans—the seasons, the year, and our aging or the recognition of important turning points. These usually occur with or without our consent. In mergings, however, we make a conscious choice for the joining to happen, to benefit those involved, and possibly others.

The myth we find ourselves enacting during merging rituals is the union of opposites, the marriage of heaven and earth, of the sacred and the mundane. This creates something larger and of a different meaning than the individual expression of two entities. It is the establishment of relatedness where before existed only distinction and difference and perhaps a recognition of polarity. It is a union that gives birth to a new whole that is, indeed, more than the sum of its parts.

A wedding is a striking example of this, but so is a corporate merger. In both cases, two individual entities choose to unite for a certain period of time for specific purposes that serve each party. In the case of "forced" mergings, it still usually centers around a choice, even though it may be between the lesser of two evils. Sharing a house to afford a more beautiful environment when one would prefer to live alone is an illustration of such a choice.

I live in a house that has an "in-law" apartment downstairs. The house is rented to me as a whole. Therefore, it is my responsibility to rent the downstairs apartment, which in some ways is a separate unit and in other ways is not. Although the apartment is sufficient unto itself, it connects to the house by a stairway just as a basement would. All utilities, upstairs and downstairs, are on a single meter. Parking is so limited that each household member must check with the others if he or she plans to have a guest drive over. And sounds—voices, music, doors closing, showers running—travel easily in a vertical as well as horizontal direction. As a result, I have had to carefully choose the downstairs tenants, as my living situation has many of the elements of communal or familial living.

When someone new moves in downstairs, no matter how I have tried to explain the situation, it generally takes time and experience for reality to sink in. We are merging two separate lifestyles, and sometimes this merging has required a series of meetings to ensure peace and harmony. Meetings and creative problem-solving can be very effective, but so too, in this situation, could a ritual.

NEW HOUSEMATES RITUAL

A ritual can also be useful in preventing some of the problems new housemates might experience.

Intention: When two people decide to share a living space, and the emotional commitment of a couple is not part of their relationship, they need something to provide assurance of harmony.

Preparation: To prepare to move into an apartment together, Lynn and Carol created a ritual that was very much like children playing house.

Manifestation: In the manifestation of this ritual, they put together a diorama of the new apartment that they named "Abode of Laughter and Beauty." They came to agreement on the purpose, use, and interior design of each room. Then they made an altar for the apartment's living room to house the diorama permanently.

Grounding: Every Monday evening they held house meetings before the altar. This served as grounding.

Whenever a merging occurs, all individuals must make adjustments to achieve a healthy and balanced relationship. A romantic involvement, a partnership, or any kind of system that is formed by the ongoing interaction between different beings is a kind of entity unto itself. A married couple, a blended family, or a team must be treated as having a reality that is part of, and yet apart from, the members that compose it.

While all rituals deal with inner or outer relationships, a merging ritual is always about specific relationships in the outer world. Accordingly, it is wise to address one of the major issues of a relationship: dependence versus independence versus interdependence. Relationships or mergings must always allow individual parties to retain their independence and distinction, even in the midst of unity. While it is valuable to be able to depend on another, it is dangerous to lose one's individual identity. That identity was struggled for and born in initiation, and if it is lost or submerged, then so, too, is the power of the union. In a merging ritual, it is important to include a focus on separateness at the same time as celebrating coming together.

Celebrate this alliance, whether based on love, common interests, or goals, as a sharing. A ritual can offer support and affirmation of commitment and can be the model for a process to work things out.

CYCLES

Cyclical celebrations are anniversaries. They are recurrences of notable events. Commemorating birthdays, wedding anniversaries, and holidays is almost a universal experience. Some celebrate the weekend—TGIF! Some even celebrate the end of the workday with "happy hour." There are always dates and times that have been important to us, and when they return, we may wish to honor them. A cyclical celebration can be just for the joy of having attained one more year. A ritual for a birthday or the anniversary of someone's death can be a time for us to reconnect. It is a time when we can recognize the depths of our emotional roots.

Emotions are a vital facet of being human, and they play an important part in rituals honoring cycles. The word *emotion* literally means "outward movement," which is apparent when we attend to the process of our feelings. Emotions allow us to move out of and beyond ourselves, as we experience when we fall in love. The rhythm of the seasons reminds us that we are in relationship with more than just other people. We are in moving, growing relationships with the life of the planet itself, with time, and with something more. Most religions have major holy days at seasonal turns, and cyclical rituals help us honor and understand patterns that are larger than ourselves. They can assist us in beginning to grasp the mystery of existence, the movements and rhythms of powers beyond our control.

Power in our lives springs from becoming more conscious and increasing the relationships among the things we have learned, so we may apply our new knowledge. At New Year's, or perhaps on birthdays, many people review the year—what they have accomplished, how they have changed—to help them set goals for the coming year. They return to the past year in a conscious way to help them in their future journeys in life. This rhythm of review, learning, and yearning moves something deeper in us that religious holidays touch on: the myth of the eternal return. As we move through life and become more conscious of who we are, we enact this myth of returning to the beginning of time in a conscious way. Much as a child moves from undifferentiated aware-ness to discrimination between self and others, we as humans move mythically from the original One at creation to differentiating between parts of that One (into our separate selves). As each of us becomes more independent and self-aware, we gain the ability to unite with others.

In this consciously chosen reunion, we can begin to contemplate the mystery of origin and feel or recognize the presence of powers larger than ourselves. This presence may be felt in the relationship celebrated at wedding anniversaries, the vitality of nature honored at seasonal festivals, or an aspect of God that is the focus of a religious holiday. This presence is an integral part of cyclical rites, as Mircea Eliade, in *Myths, Dreams, and Mysteries* (Harper & Row, 1957), explains: "the World is not only re-established and regenerated, but is also sanctified by the symbolic presence of the Immortals....The Immortals make it stable, healthy, rich and holy, as it was at the beginning of Time."

A WINTER SOLSTICE RITUAL

This larger presence may be felt in the vitality of nature honored at seasonal festivals or as an aspect of the Creator celebrated in a religious holiday.

Intention: Each December, we hold a Yule open house, with the customary tree-trimming, gift-giving, delicious food, and warm feelings. We also include a wassail ritual. Wassail is an old Anglo-Saxon winter drink, spicy, hot, and hearty, whose name means "wholeness."

Preparation: After all the guests arrive and socialize for a bit, four or five of us work together in the kitchen to assemble this amazing brew.

Manifestation: We carry the wassail out to the accompaniment of bells and horns and set it before the blazing fireplace. As we pass a specially prepared log-shaped loaf of Yule bread among the guests, we talk about the year, the increasing darkness from fall to winter, and the inward searching that accompanies the season. We urge all the guests to recognize an aspect of self that is no longer of use, that perhaps they have recently noticed interfering in how they would choose to live their lives. When they feel ready to release this way of being, they walk up to the hearth and throw a bit of their Yule bread into the flames, symbolically offering the outmoded part of themselves to the cleansing fire. We then toast the return of the light and the wholeness and unity arising from the darkness and isolation of winter. We feed one another a bit of Yule bread to give, receive, and ground symbolically the gift of Spirit from the wassail, the symbol of the One.

Grounding: Discussion, singing, feasting, and merriment follow in good spirit.

ENDINGS

In an ending something has terminated: a relationship, a job, a project, or even a life. A sense of relief or satisfaction may occur, or a great sense of loss and emptiness may transpire. Suddenly being without something that was an integral part of our life can cause us to feel completely ungrounded. An ending without a sense of completion implies being unfinished rather than being settled. We have more issues to deal with when things end against our wishes than when we purposefully conclude something in our lives. For instance, a death, particularly of a child, leaves you to deal not only with your grief, but also with the hopes and dreams you had for that person and all the things you were never able to share with each other. The rituals of wakes and funerals are very important in helping to cope with such loss. Our culture also provides rituals such as retirement dinners or bon voyage parties for less devastating endings, but many other endings could benefit from a ritual.

One such powerful situation leaving painful and possibly unresolvable issues could be returning from a business trip to find your home empty. The furniture is gone; the children are gone; your spouse is gone.

Nothing remains but a few of your personal items. There is no note, and you find your spouse unavailable to you. You may not be able ever to understand what happened if you are forced to deal with this alone.

Whether the endings in your life have unresolved elements or have intentional completion, you must still establish where you stand after the dust settles. It is important to recognize that no matter what passes, you remain. However, who you are has changed. A large part of your experience of yourself is a composite of all your experiences, synthesized by your responses to them. If you take a moment, you may be able to recall the homes in which you lived over the years and what life was like at each of these places. Perhaps you can remember special moments of love given or received. Each warm memory still available to you has helped shape you, has given you strength and character, has affected your values and perceptions.

To recover these legacies, you need time and the ability to integrate an ending transition in a way that enriches you and honors what has ended. A ritual in the form of a memorial can support you in the important process of grieving.

Sometimes in grief, you may find an ocean of loss so deep it seems bottomless, with waves so fierce they threaten to annihilate you. When these feelings surface, your personal emotion has accessed the archetype of sorrow. You are living the myth of separation, of the loss of union with the primal, undifferentiated One: the myth of manifestation from a sacred world of relatedness into a material world of duality, the story of the fall from Eden. This deepening of emotion is most often seen in the death of a spouse, in which the original joining echoed the movement of conscious return to something larger, as discussed in the "Mergings" section of this chapter. Losses of this magnitude in a person's life always touch off questions about the meaning of life, and while it is difficult to explore these questions in your pain, grief does provide an opportunity to truly deepen your understanding of existence.

It is through suffering that we learn compassion, that we recognize a bond common to all people. We can experience the paradox of being united in our loss and separation, and in that experience know that we are not separate. Most religions agree that death, as the completion of life on earth, opens the possibility of a life with conscious union with the Tao, with God, with Goddess, with Spirit, that is improbable for all but a few holy persons while we are in human form. Ideally, we complete what we need to do on earth before death ends our lives; if not, the Hindu reincarnates or the Christian spends time in purgatory before ultimate reunion with the One.

While the death of a loved one brings the fullest experience of this archetype, the myth is present and available to us in all losses, at all completions. Whether to deepen our experience of the archetype or to make living the myth more bearable, a ritual of completion is most valuable.

A DIVORCE RITUAL

Jenny came to us for help developing a ritual to help her cope with her divorce. During the year following her breakup with John, she had worked hard in therapy. With great courage, she had faced and coped with her loss, her rage, her guilt, her fear, her sense of powerlessness. After nine months, she felt stronger than ever before and liked her life, her work, and her relationships. As the divorce decision approached, Jenny began feeling sad and scared. When the divorce was granted, many of her feelings from the split with John recurred or intensified. Her emotional work of the previous year made the divorce easier to deal with, but it was difficult to finalize what had happened. Together we worked out an ending ritual for her to do at home.

Preparation: Jenny took a day for herself. She cleaned the house and took a shower. She gathered the materials she decided to use in her ritual and stated her intention: "Today I say good-bye to an old way of being and embrace a new life."

Manifestation: Jenny looked through pictures of their wedding and of their life together. She read over John's love letters and wept. Then she wrote a letter to the relationship they had shared, giving thanks for their love and growth and forgiveness for the hurts they caused each other. She added this letter to those from John and tied them carefully together with a fresh ribbon. As she placed this bundle and the wedding pictures into a special box to keep the memories safe, Jenny said good-bye to their marriage and their old way of relating.

Lighting a fire in the fireplace, Jenny burned their marriage certificate. As the paper turned to fire and smoke, she set free the false beliefs and expectations she still held for the marriage and from the divorce: "I let go of the belief that I am not worthy of love. I am a loving being, deserving of love." She drank a sip of juice to help make that belief a living part of her. "I let go of expecting our relationship to make me a whole person. I am a whole person unto myself."

Grounding: When she finished her list and her juice, she stretched and thanked God for her life, for the love she had experienced, for her strength, for the depth of her emotions, and for her growth. A sadness was still present, but a fullness, and a new joy in life, existed as well.

Ending rituals can help us deal with retirement, menopause, divorce, leaving home, death, or even the loss of body parts (due to an accident or to surgery such as a mastectomy). This category deals with the emotions that are most painful. The rituals must contain delicacy, patience, and compassion.

HEALINGS

All rituals that move toward balance and increase conscious relatedness in an ethical way are healing rituals. Beginning rituals help balance the fearful transition between an old and a new way of being. Merging rituals help balance and enlarge the relationship between two separate entities. Cyclical rituals help us balance our lives by increased understanding of our relationships with time and with other larger forces. Ending rituals offer us a way to deal with the polarities of life and death; they provide us an approach to understanding questions fundamental to human nature and the nature of existence. Whenever we touch the energies that fuel and direct life, healing can happen.

When an imbalance exists in your life—a physical illness, an emotional upheaval, a way of thinking that interferes with living fully, an intensity of concern, or a state of apathy that threatens your soul—ritual can help. Healing rituals offer a time for you to be fully present with the pain as well as a means to finding acceptance of it.

We often spend incredible amounts of time and energy fighting what is really happening. For change to occur, we must admit what is true and accept it, even if it is unpleasant. According to James Hillman in *Suicide and the Soul* (Spring Publications, 1964), "health, like wholeness, is completion in individuality, and to this belongs the dark side of life as well: symptoms, suffering, tragedy, and death. *Wholeness and health there-fore do not exclude these 'negative' phenomena;* they are requisite for health." When resistance to the existence of this dark side of reality is relieved, the tyranny of pain diminishes and change can occur. Balance can then be restored.

A RITUAL FOR PLANETARY HEALING

This ritual feels increasingly important to us as changes in the world reflect so much fear.

Intention: To restore the earth, the environment, and all living things to a state of health.

Preparation: A few of us gather weekly at noon, the time of the most light. We sit quietly in a circle, focusing on our breath, allowing distractions to be released while exhaling and strength and centered-ness to enter when inhaling.

Manifestation: The leader for the week lights a white candle in the center of our circle and states our intention: that we gather to promote healing on and of our planet earth, for the good of all. We stand and join hands, and the leader guides us through a meditation in which we each become filled with light, acknowledging our individual wounds and imbalances, then imagining ourselves well and whole. We let the light expand from us and fill and embrace our circle, and we speak the names of those people we know who need healing, imagining them in the center of the light circle, seeing them move toward balance. We pray in this way for world leaders, global areas of strife or injustice, pollution—each time imagining the way things are now and then the way they can be. After this, we lift up our arms and send this globe of healing energy out into the universe, asking that it be used where it might best be of service. We close by giving thanks to Spirit and hugs to one another.

Grounding: The sense of peace and healing from the ritual is carried home with each of the participants; we can call on it throughout the week to help those qualities become part of our daily activities.

This ritual often leaves us feeling in love with the world, and definite similarities exist between healing and love. They are not things we can create, but things that happen to us and through us, states that we are blessed to experience. Love and healing are energies that exist, awaiting access, and when the proper avenues are created for them, these energies pour through and grace us with their expression. Ritual can be such an avenue.

SELF EXPLORATION

Reflect on the following questions to get a sense of how transitions have impacted you throughout your life. Use your journal to note your memories, thoughts, and feelings.

1. Turning Points. Think about the different turning points you have experienced in your life. Ritual will have marked some, but not others. What were some of your most important life transitions?

2. Choose one of these turning points to explore. How were you affected? Did you use ritual? How did the ritual affect your process? How can you imagine ritual would have been useful if ritual did not mark this time?

3. Into which category—Beginnings, Mergings, Cyclical Events, Endings, or Healings—does your current transition best fit?

4. In creating a ritual for this transition, what would your intention be?

At the end of the week, read over your journal entries. Write down what you learned and anything new you notice from reading through your experiences this week.

CHAPTER 4

the process of ritual

The process of ritual follows the same basic stages we experience in life. These stages of unfolding are paralleled by the seasons and their changes. In spring, the increased warmth of the earth awakens seeds to life, and the sprouts struggle upward. During summer, the nourishment of the sun, water, and earth helps the seedlings find a more mature form, and the plants may produce exquisite flowers. After pollination in the fall, fruit drops to the ground or is harvested. In winter, we eat the fruits and save the seeds, or the fallen seeds find their way into the earth to await the recurrence of spring.

Each of the seasons and each age of a plant—seedling, sapling, flower, and fruit—is unique. But when we look at the whole cycle of the year or of a plant's growth, we see the larger beauty of balance and rhythm inherent in creation and in life.

When we create something—a dinner, a painting, a ritual—we go through the same process. We are inspired and we bring that inspiration into creation by thinking and planning. As we work with our ideas and the feelings they evoke, the inspiration finds a skeletal form. That form provides a framework to flesh out. This is all part of the preparation process, and the manifestation process echoes the same stages. Let's look at how we might express this process in the example of preparing a dinner for some friends.

Intention: An old friend is in town with his new girlfriend. You want to cook dinner for them as a way to honor your friend and welcome his partner. This is the inspiration for the dinner.

Preparation: You think about the kinds of food he likes, rummage through cookbooks for recipes, and toy with ideas for table settings. You decide that while you'd like to serve filet mignon, your budget is better suited to beef Stroganoff. It might be nice to create a more inviting atmosphere with music and flowers, and you consider the mood that would be most appropriate.

As you play with these ideas, different feelings begin to emerge. Perhaps you're nervous about what kind of impression you'll make on his new love. What if you don't like her? Are you jealous? Will your friends think you don't value them enough to take them out to dinner? You worry a little, then decide to put candles on the dinner table for elegance and warmth. You work through each of your doubts and fears until you return to your original intention of welcoming these people into your home and into your heart. Finally, you begin to feel more relaxed about creating a successful evening, then—oh, no! You remember the girlfriend is a committed vegetarian. This requires more research to decide on a suitable entree. It's clear now that the plans you made in the creative stage are taking form.

Manifestation: Your next step is to bring these forms into manifestation. You make a grocery list, make special stops at the bakery and flower stand after the market, and return home to prepare. The afternoon is spent cleaning, polishing, arranging the table, and cooking. When things are almost complete, you take some time to shower and dress. When your guests arrive, you greet them genially and escort them into the living room for hors d'oeuvres. This is the physical beginning of your dinner. As you move into the dining room for the meal, you further the intention and mood of the evening by lighting the candles and making a toast to friendships old and new. During the dinner your rapport increases with the sharing of good food, a bottle of wine, and warm conversation. After the meal ends, everyone lingers over coffee, listening to music and talking. Eventually, the evening draws to a close.

Grounding: As you say good-bye, you all promise to keep in touch. The dinner has been successful, and you feel good as you clean up. The next day you talk with your friend about the evening and make plans for the three of you to get together again.

PREPARATION
Preparing a ritual involves four stages: clarifying the intention, planning, emotional process, and physical preparation. We describe the steps of each stage here and outline them in the Ritual Worksheet in Chapter 8: Ritual Guidelines and Worksheet.

CLARIFYING THE INTENTION
The primary differences between the dinner described above and a ritual dinner are the conscious carrying and implementation of the intention through each stage of the process. Identifying, clarifying, and

developing the intention are the first stage of preparation. The following are some questions to consider:

* Why are you thinking about doing a ritual? What has happened, is happening, or is about to happen that inspires you?

* What is the purpose of this ritual? What do you want it to accomplish? What kind of mood do you want created? Whom will this ritual affect? How will this ritual benefit the participants?

* What myth or archetypal journey might be similar to the inspiration for your ritual?

* Is the aim of this ritual realistic? If you find you have many different goals, you may need to do several different rituals.

* Of the five ritual categories—Beginnings, Mergings, Cycles, Endings, or Healings—which seems most appropriate? How?

Go to Chapter 3: Types of Rituals, and reread the section on the category you have chosen. Make sure you can clearly state your intention.

PLANNING

Having clarified your intention, now progress to the planning stage. This stage encompasses choosing different symbols and actions for each Element of ritual (Earth, Air, Fire, Water, and Essence; see Chapter 5: The Elements of Ritual), creative design, and logistics.

Once you determine what kind of ritual you wish to create, you need to decide on the following:

* Who should participate in this ritual, and why? Do the people who will be involved in the ritual have the same aim? What purpose do they have in common? If you do this ritual alone, are you ambivalent about achieving your goal? If so, what belief or idea do you need to let go of or work through? Is there anyone who might be touched by but would not benefit from the performance of this ritual? If so, how can you shift the intention so that your aim is clear and no one could be hurt?

* What specifically do you want to recognize, honor, support, or heal?

* When would be most appropriate to enact this ritual?

* Where would be the most fitting setting for the ritual to take place?

* How will this ritual benefit and affect the participants?

* How much or how little do you need to do?

CHOOSING SYMBOLS

Chapter 5: The Elements of Ritual will give you a thorough understanding of the four Elements—Earth, Air, Fire, and Water—and of the unifying principle of Essence. By combining this information with what you learned about symbols from Chapter 2: Myth, History, and Symbol, you should be able to choose symbols that are meaningful, powerful, relevant, and that bring a sense of balance and wholeness to your ritual. For now, just be aware that Earth is generally associated with the body, the direction of north, the Jungian function of sensation, and in the tarot, with the princesses. The grounding stage of a ritual, and ending rituals, falls in the realms of Earth.

"When the statement is made that what is great must be right, it means not that great and right are two different things, but that without rightness there is no greatness. The relations of heaven and earth are never other than great and right."

—Richard Wilhelm,
I Ching

The Element of Air corresponds to the mind, the direction of east, the function of thinking, and the princes in the tarot. Rituals of merging, and the planning stage of a ritual, relate to Air.

Fire generally relates to what is called spirit or inspiration, which we are going to call energy. Fire also corresponds to the direction of south, the function of intuition, and the kings. Rituals that honor beginnings, and the ritual stage of inspiration, fit into this category.

Water's relationships are emotions, the west, feelings, and the queens. The stages of emotional process and blessings belong with Water, as do cyclical types of rituals.

The fifth Element of Spirit—here called Essence—is not included in all systems. We suggest that this Element be understood as that which is the foundation for and yet transcends all the other Elements. Essence is present in the ritual as a whole and in the larger energies that enter the ceremony. Healing rituals correspond to the Element of Essence.

When you have a sense of what symbols you would like to incorporate into your ritual, you can focus more on the creative design.

Creative Design

Ritual is a performance art. Allowing yourself to have artistic license, to let ideas flow no matter how extravagant or odd they may seem, puts you in the most creative space. You may need to start by recalling what a traditional ceremony for this occasion includes (if there is one), and spin off from there. For example, a birthday party celebrates the anniversary of the day someone is born. You invite people who are glad to know that this person successfully made it through another year. There is generally a cake with a candle to mark each year that has passed and one extra to grow on. Blowing out the candles and making a wish for the coming year relate to taking the strength and wisdom acquired over the past years and creating a positive intention with it that the person will use inwardly as a guiding light. At children's parties, along with the birthday song, may come birthday spankings—one for each year—related to the pain of growing. Lastly, gifts are an expression of love from each of the guests.

An example of a birthday ritual follows:

Intention: For my fortieth birthday, I decided to perform a ritual that would include some of the standard symbols, but with the intention of expressing what being forty meant to me.

Preparation: I decided to rent a space that was large enough to accommodate all of my friends and my family—everyone who had supported me through the years and was still in my life. Each person was asked to bring, as a "giveaway," an item that represented their personal gift to the world or something they liked about themselves.

Manifestation: During the ritual, everyone stood encircling a round loaf of bread, which held a single candle to represent unity. I expressed my feelings about my belief that the first half of life involves discovering something about who you are and what your gifts are and that the second half has more of an outward focus, sharing your gifts to make a better world. I described what I felt my gift was and explained the symbolic object I'd brought to represent it. I then passed my gift to the person to my left, who did the same with her gift, and so on around the circle until all gifts were shared. We then did a short meditation, holding hands, focusing on how, by being who we are and sharing it with those around us, we create something that continues to grow and spread. We mentally released any limitations that might keep us from sharing our personal gifts or resources. Finally, we all stepped forward to take and eat a piece of the bread, which symbolized the grounding and nurturing of what had been shared.

Grounding: The rest of the ritual included many of the traditional elements of a birthday celebration, but the way it had been personalized gave it a meaning that has stayed with me to this day. When the ritual you want to perform has no model that already exists, you may still find similar elements in other ceremonies that might give you ideas. Basically, you need to consider the following:

* How will you start?

* Will you include music, poetry, chants, readings, speeches, or meditations?

* Will you include a cleansing of the people or of the space?

* Will you include the use of food or wine for feasting or offerings?

* How will all the symbols best be included?

* Will there be any particular artistic event, such as body-painting, mask-making, incense-crafting, the making of a ritual object, or something along those lines?

* How will you sustain the pace?

* What kind of ending would be fitting?

You need to consider these kinds of questions, keeping in mind the intention and the symbols you have chosen. As you sketch out your ideas, you'll find that the next section enters the picture.

Logistics

Here you want to consider each person's role and responsibilities in the ritual, plan the gathering and organizing of materials, and work out the timing. You may want to have a planning meeting with the participants if each will have a very active role. If you will do most of the leading, it may only be necessary to contact the guests, discuss what they need to bring, get an idea of how they will participate, and then coordinate everything. If others will be a part of the ritual, getting feedback from them will give you valuable information about what to add or delete.

If you are performing this ritual alone, you still need to spend some time with this stage, as the preparation stages all enhance the power of the ritual itself.

EMOTIONAL PROCESS

The limitations you dealt with in your planning stage may have raised some emotions, such as anger, frustration, excitement, or doubt. In every creative process, you run into blocks, and creating a ritual is no exception. This is an excellent opportunity to take stock of yourself, to see if your original goals remain the same, and to explore any doubts or fears that may come forth. If the ritual you are planning is a celebration, you may find yourself tapping into a lot of positive and warm feelings. Should the celebration be for yourself, however, beware of the old "Do I really deserve this?" plague.

When the ritual is to help deal with illness, death, or some painful ending, it is more likely that some difficult feelings will emerge. Dealing with these feelings is a cleansing and part of the healing process of ritual. It is important to acknowledge and honor whatever emotions arise. Include symbolic events in the ritual that will assist you in releasing some of the more difficult feelings. Do this by safely burning or burying paper that names certain things or feelings or even by burning or burying certain objects or photographs from which you wish to be freed. Remember, each of the Elements offers symbolic ways to find release.

PREPARATION
This is the time to actually gather the necessary materials, set up, and make sure all the details worked out in the planning stage are coming together. You may want a checklist to ensure that each necessary item is covered. This stage feels a lot like packing for a vacation, and in a sense, it is quite similar. You are taking all the essential things to go away to another time and place in which your ordinary reality is temporarily set aside and everything is designed to offer healing or renewal.

MANIFESTATION
The manifestation stage is the performance of the ritual. Four parts exist to this: creating a sacred space, declaration and enactment of the intention, invocation of larger energies, and blessing and closure.

CREATING A SACRED SPACE
After you gather and prepare all the materials as needed, you must define and consecrate the space in which you will perform the ritual. If the space is indoors, you might want to clear away some of the things that ordinarily identify its use. Clean or straighten up and then decorate the space or set up the things you plan to use during the ritual. A

typical cleansing involves burning incense, or some dried herbs such as sage or sweetgrass, and letting the smoke fill the room, changing the energy with its pungency. If you are performing your ritual outdoors, you may need to delineate the area to contain the ritual with rocks, chairs, or something that helps you feel a sense of enclosure. Describing the sacred space in the shape of a circle helps induce a sense of wholeness and unity. Whether the ritual will be indoors or outdoors, there should be some indication that when one enters the ritual space, things are different and special in comparison to the surrounding area. You can partially accomplish this with some form of ceremonial entry.

DECLARATION AND ENACTMENT OF INTENTION

Once people formally enter the ritual space and take their places, the mood of the ritual is formed, and the intention is declared. Many formal events begin with a greeting or welcome, followed by some form of introduction that includes the purpose or intention. In a wedding, for example, the officiant often states, "Dearly beloved, we are gathered here today to witness and celebrate the joining in marriage of these two people." One of the most common places we see this structure is on television. The function of the host or emcee of a TV show greets and welcomes the viewers, audience, and possibly the guests and then proceeds to describe the events that are to follow. The show is then presented according to the stated outline.

And so it is with a ritual. You have already determined what you want your ritual to include and have developed a plan and some form of agenda. This is when all of these things are carried out.

"The idea of a receptacle is an archetypal idea…. It is the idea of the magic circle which is drawn round something that has to be prevented from escaping or protected against hostile influences…. When the ground-plan for a city was set out, there used to be a ritual walk or ride round the circumferences in order to protect the place within…. This structure of a circle within a square is called in Sanskrit a Mandala…. The symbol of the Mandala has exactly this meaning of a holy place, a 'tenemos' to protect the centre…."

—C. G. Jung,
Analytical Psychology,
Its Theory and Practice

INVOCATION AND DIRECTION OF LARGER ENERGIES

One thing that makes a ritual different from a TV show is that the mistress or master of ceremonies is conducting a sacred ceremony.

To assist in the process of shifting from the secular to the sacred, invoke energies that are greater than yourself to be with you during the rite. Even though these energies may be called from within, as when connecting with the God of your heart or your sense of your Spirit, they are transpersonal rather than personal. Also call for the expression of an archetype, such as Venus, the goddess of love, to support an anniversary, or an ancestor or historical figure to bring, say, the energy of the wise elder. Call on Element, quality, or direction with a formal greeting and beckoning: "Hail, O East, direction of sunrise, new light, and beginnings…" or "Mother Earth, lend us your strength, support, and nurturing as we…. " In a traditional religious ceremony, you call on God, Allah, the Creator of the universe, or in whatever/whomever you believe, to bless and guide you in the ritual.

Invoke energies with words or with actions. The simple act of lighting a candle can represent bringing in Spirit, or light, as a conscious force. Whatever you decide to do, it is important to hold the intention of what you wish to accomplish as you take this step. It is also important to remember that calling in larger energies can be intimidating for some people. After all, you are calling on a force that in some way has a greater, or at least a different kind of, power from the one you are generally aware of having yourself. Do this with honor and respect, and do not attempt to call forth anything that might be associated with anger, fear, or danger. It is unlikely that you will confront danger if you do not provoke it.

BLESSING AND CLOSURE

The final stages of the ritual confirm and summarize as well as complete what has been done. A semitraditional wedding ceremony exemplifies this:

> *May these two find in each other the love for which all seek. May they grow in understanding and compassion. May the home they establish together be such a place of love that many will find there a neighbor and a friend.... Inasmuch as _____ and _____ have consented together in marriage and have witnessed the same before this company, and thereto have pledged their faith to the other, and have declared the same by joining hands, and by giving and receiving a ring, they are husband and wife together. Those whom love hath joined together, let none put asunder.*

Certainly all endings need not be as formal. In fact, in a ritual that is totally personal, with no one else in attendance, you may choose not to speak out loud at all. Many rituals are completed with only symbolic actions, such as leaving food as an offering, extinguishing candles, burning a photograph, ending a musical piece, or getting a hug from everyone in attendance.

Another consideration at this stage is what you do with the energies you have invoked. This is an appropriate occasion to thank the forces that be for attending, guarding, or assisting and then release them to return to their own realm. You might also ask that the love and good feelings shared by those present be carried out to touch the hearts of others in their lives.

A simple rule for this part of the process might be: whatever is opened must be closed; whatever is called in must be released; whatever is started must be brought full circle to completion.

GROUNDING

The purpose of grounding is to evaluate the experience and integrate the effects of the ritual. The first steps are breaking down the space and evaluating what transpired during the ceremony. The next stages are integrating and actualizing the changes.

BREAKDOWN AND EVALUATION

The last stage of the ritual carries over into the beginning stages of completion. The physical area must be seen to, the sacred space returned to normal, and the ritual tools put away. As you attend to the physical acts of completion, you may notice that a somewhat different you is acting. You should evaluate the shifts that have occurred in you or in the other participants. Assess the changes that have taken place by considering questions such as the following:

* What was especially moving, exciting, frightening, healing, affirming, or provocative?

* Have any of the relationships shifted, such as with those present, an individual with their inner Self, or an individual with someone not present?

* How, specifically, do you feel?

* What, if anything, was learned?

Sometimes it is difficult to articulate the changes until some time has passed. Keep monitoring yourself over the next days and weeks to note anything that feels related to your ritual work. Journal entries can be especially useful for this aspect.

You can also benefit from evaluating the ritual itself. Consider the objects used as symbols, the performance, and the design to determine what worked well and what you could improve on or discard. Each ritual helps you better prepare for the next.

INTEGRATION AND ACTUALIZATION

The last stage of completion is to follow through with any inspiration you may have received from the ritual. You may have discovered something in the course of the ritual that you can carry over into your daily life. When you are caught up in the energy and magic of a ceremony, profound feelings or insights may arise. The ritual may even have afforded you the opportunity to experience some new and welcomed behaviors. Although the sacred quality of the ritual may lead you to believe that what has occurred in that time belongs only to that time, the truth is that the rareness of the occasion may have left you with special and valuable gifts.

A healing ritual might teach you that you need some time for meditation or to be listened to. A ritual for beginnings may have taught you new ways to deal with fear. Being the leader of a ritual may have taught you to recognize your power from the ability to empower others. Whatever you learned, the value increases as you find ways to incorporate these gifts into your life.

SELF EXPLORATION

The following questions will help you with the process of creating rituals for important events in your life. Use your journal to note your responses.

1. Write about how the ritual process described in this chapter appears in other creative projects in your life.

2. Think about a ritual you have performed. Use the questions presented in this chapter to review the ritual. How would using this process guide have improved the ritual?

3. Think about a ritual you would like to or are planning to perform. Answer the questions presented in this chapter to help further your process.

At the end of the week, read over your journal entries. Write down what you learned and anything new you notice from reading through your experiences this week.

CHAPTER 5

the elements of ritual

We have spoken repeatedly about the importance of balance. The purpose of ritual is to increase balance and connection within ourselves, with one another, with the world, and with the subtle but powerful rhythms and energies of the cosmos and the spiritual realm. To achieve balance in a complex whole, we must be familiar with the component parts, recognize the way each is or can be expressed, and know when one Element or another is preventing equilibrium.

We are all physical, feeling, thinking, inspired human beings. Each of us tends to be more at ease with the qualities of some of these aspects than others. When we meet people who are working to develop those areas of themselves with which they are less facile and have achieved a fair balance, we say they are "well rounded" or "well adjusted" or that they have "gotten themselves together."

An imbalanced individual would be a "Mr. Spock" type—someone with extraordinary analytical ability, incredibly brilliant, yet with an apparent lack of feeling that makes him seem not quite human. You may know someone who can express amazing depth of feeling through music or painting, but trips over her tongue when trying to converse. How about a person so involved in the dreams of what might be or of what could happen that he is boggled by the practical world and the minutiae of daily living?

"The pentacle is the four elements plus the fifth—essence. And it is the five stages of life, each an aspect of the Goddess:
1. Birth…(beginning),
2. Initiation…(individuation),
3. Love…(union),
4. Repose…(integration), and
5. Death…(letting go)."

—Starhawk,
The Spiral Dance

An individual as imbalanced as those in the exaggerated examples above is like a table with one short leg. In a healing ritual, helping someone become more aware of his or her essential imbalances may be the first step toward wholeness.

During times of transition, we may find ourselves out of balance in other ways. A difficult passage may catapult us into an overwhelming emotional state, or it may have the opposite effect. Some people are so afraid of their feelings that after a crisis, which may cause them to shut down and become very rational and contained, as we all have a tendency to do, they hide in that protected condition. The different inner states have correspondences in Elements, seasons, directions, symbols, colors, and more. A ritual provides an allegorical mirror in which the balance created in the ceremony can reflect on our inner state.

THE ELEMENTS

The following are some of the correspondences that you can symbolically use to help create balance:

East	South	West	North
spring	summer	autumn	winter
Air	*Fire*	*Water*	*Earth*
infancy	youth	middle age	old age
dawn	*midday*	*evening*	*night*
crescent moon	full moon	waning moon	new moon
thinking	*intuition*	*feeling*	*sensation*

Notice that only four Elements are represented in this chart. The fifth Element, Essence, is the energy that permeates all nature and represents the wholeness or unity itself.

We experience the Elements daily in our lives. The sun (Fire) and the stars at night radiate their light and heat, which travel through our atmosphere (Air) and the oceans (Water), which cover a large portion of the solid world (Earth).

The relationship among these four Elements is Essence, which we perceive in the interactions and movements arising from Elemental relationships. A sunset, for example, is the relationship of light from the sun (Fire) moving through the atmosphere (Air) and clouds (Water) and registering on the retinas of our eyes (Earth). This physical sensation (Earth) evokes feelings (Water)—"Wow!"—and thoughts (Air)—"How beautiful!"—in us. The sight may also inspire (Fire) us to say a prayer of thanks, to try to capture the image on canvas, or just to carry the energy of the event with us through the rest of the evening.

The Elements are ever present in our lives. Increasing our awareness of them allows us to experience a sense of sacredness more fully, which is vital to ritual. Let's explore each Element in greater detail.

FIRE (INTUITION) △

The Element of Fire in the Jungian typology is associated with intuition. Through this function, we experience visions or new possibilities. According to June Singer in *Boundaries of the Soul* (Anchor Press, 1973), the tendency of intuition is to allow us "to gain a total impression of a situation and also a sense for where it is leading, that is, for what may become of it." Intuition leads us to the quest. "Because he [the intuitive or fiery type] is always seeking out new possibilities, stable conditions suffocate him. He seizes new objects or situations with great intensity, sometimes with extraordinary enthusiasm...." writes Joseph Campbell in *The Portable Jung* (Viking Press, 1971). You might say that each new situation is an initiation into another level of growth.

This kind of fiery inspiration is also related to spirit. The fifth Element, Essence, may be seen as Spirit too, but with a capital *S*. Fire may be understood as the first emanation from the ineffable essence of Spirit. It is trans-temporal. The spirit of Fire can be expressed simply as warmth or more dramatically as passion. Fire also symbolizes faith, will, force, and courage. In a ritual we might express this with a cone of power, in which the energy is increasingly raised in the circle until the force is so great that a climactic release and subsequent cleansing occur.

"Getting the Holy Spirit" is a way Fire is embodied in the religious rituals used by some churches, such as the Pentecostal Church. Raising the kundalini is another way of incorporating the fiery energy of spirit.

To symbolize this energy in a ritual, you may use a wand, or candles, or a fire for cleansing or burning away things that must be released. Actions may include anything that inflames or inspires. In a ritual that represents beginnings, Fire might symbolize leadership, inspiration, or the quest. The qualities of passion or enthusiasm might be the focus in a merging ritual. A cyclical celebration might honor aspiration or the challenge of another turn of time's wheel. You might evoke will or strength to help with an ending. Healing rituals might benefit from expressing Fire as optimism or purification.

AIR (MIND) △

Our minds provide us with the experience of objectivity and discrimination. Through the mind, we can notice differences, make comparisons, categorize, and name things. You might say we look at the relationships among things. We can gain information, understanding, and clarity using our mind or our intellect. This process of thought is associated with Air. Perhaps this is because our thoughts are so much like the sky—either clear and open; clear with small, white clouds streaking across or drifting casually by; or dark and heavy, tormented by threatening gray-black thunderclouds. Our thoughts may be like the rushing winds of a tornado, expressing our rage or blinding us with our confusion. The Air is also a medium that carries the expressions of thought as the waves of sound or as the signals from radio or television.

In a ritual, we express the Element of Air in communication, ideas, meditations, and possibilities. In time, Air is associated with the future. Methods of expression can be speech, song, storytelling, poetry, chanting, and drumming. Air can be symbolized by things representative of thought, such as books, or by objects that find the air as home: incense, feathers, or petals, which we can toss to the wind in a ritual. Swords or knives cut through or discriminate, and so also betoken Air. The drums that produce the powerful rhythmic sound waves that provide the vehicle for journeying can also symbolize Air.

When we symbolically denote Air in a ritual, we do so for a number of reasons. In honoring or invoking Air, we ask the qualities represented by it to be available to us. In a ritual that falls into the category of beginnings, we may use Air to represent original thinking and help tap into new ideas. In a merging ritual, we may use Air to let us recognize the differences between the individuals and create ways to understand and communicate that allow the distinctions to remain. Air can help us to see the gestalt, or larger picture, in which all parts have a place. Using the Element of Air in a cyclical celebration can help us reflect on the past and understand patterns that occur. In an ending ritual, we can symbolically use Air for release when it is necessary or to help remember, when retaining a part of what has been lost is what we need. Bringing Air into a healing may mean undoing the negative mental processes that created defeat, futility, indecisiveness, overanalysis, or self-criticism.

WATER (FEELINGS) ▽

Our feelings afford us a sense of rhythm and relatedness. Sometimes, looking at a sleeping child or seeing a sky streaked with the reds and oranges of a setting sun, you can feel as touched as if you've been blessed by some unseen force. That feeling can move you out of a sense of isolation into one of connection with other people or with nature.

When you feel that recognition of sentience with another, you may experience joy and love; when you feel distant or separated from a person you love, you may become hurt or angry. Even anger is in relation to someone or something, and it usually comes when the known rhythm of that relationship has been upset.

Feelings, like Water, can have many forms. Some are held obscure and protected in hidden parts of our psyches, like water that has seeped down to the deepest level and formed a dark pool. Cold, contained feelings can give the effect of ice; slow anger may seem like steam; overwhelming grief, sadness, or helplessness can whip you about like a violent hurricane; and the feelings of contentment that come from being well loved may remind you of the clear, sparkling, reflective qualities of a pristine lake. And just as you can look into the smooth surface of a body of water and see the likeness of an image, so Water symbolizes illusion. It connects us with the past.

In rituals, we use water and other liquids to indicate feelings. We also find feeling present in the movements and emotions of the participants and in the cadence and rhythm of the process of the ritual itself. We often use chalices as a symbol for Water. Washing or sprinkling water for cleansing is a common ritual expression. Water is the receptive Element, and we may use it in beginning rituals to express openness to something new. In a merging ritual, we may use Water as a symbol of harmony or empathy. A cyclical celebration can employ the Element of Water to convey the sense of flow that occurs as we pass through time. When honoring an ending, the Element of Water might signify assimilation, sentiment, or sensitivity. The Element of Water can bring the qualities of compassion and nurturing into a healing ritual.

EARTH (BODY) ▽

We are earthbound because of our bodies. Of the Elemental expressions, Earth is the least able to move freely. We must treat it with honor and patience. There is no doubt that our thoughts, feelings, and intuitions are commonly held in check by the physical process that contains them. Our bodies are vehicles of experience. They provide a way for us to express ourselves and to ground or manifest our energies, in addition to allowing access to the experience of sensation. Our involvement with Earth gives us a sense of the present.

The earth itself is recognized as a great body of land or as the fruitful Mother Earth. This was exemplified by the Romans, who engraved their tombstones with the phrase *Mater genuit, Mater recepit*, which translates as "The Mother bore me, the Mother took me back."

The information we have of ancient peoples and their ways from monuments cleft on the earth, cut into the earth, or sealed in the heart of it illustrates one of the reasons the Element of Earth is associated with heritage, history, and the legacies of our ancestors. Even our physical bodies give indication of our ancestry through genetic traits.

The information we have from the past guides us in building the present and the future. Building is associated with the Earth, as are the qualities associated with creation and construction. So patience, endurance, determination, and practicality are all Earthy considerations.

When you wish to represent the Element of Earth in a ritual, accent the concepts of grounding, stability, solidity, and security. You might choose symbolic objects such as stones, metals, crystals, or food. A ritual to honor beginnings may emphasize determination or work on grounding the emerging energies. In a cyclical celebration, you may want to explore the idea of what you have gained over time. You may wish to highlight patience in a merging ceremony. The Element of Earth can target heritage or legacy in rituals for endings. For healing, address stability through Earth. Earth can be symbolically represented in many ways—through the making of fetishes or talismans, with masks, feasting, planting, harvesting, or sculpting.

ESSENCE (LIFE FORCE ENERGY) ☉

The function of Essence in a ritual is to create balance and unity. Because this is also the function of ritual, Essence is present in the ritual itself. Consciously blending the four Elements of a ritual in a balanced way also gives rise to Essence—the whole that is more than the sum of its parts.

Even though Essence is present in the ritual itself, it is useful—we think vital—to include a symbolic expression of this life force energy. As it is made sensible, the reality of a presence otherwise easily disregarded can have profound impact. Recognizing Essence is the vehicle toward transcendence. Although many names may exist for this quintessential energy—*prana, chi*, ether, Akasha, Spirit, God, the Tao, to name some—this force, so fundamental, is still just an abstract principle to most.

Therefore, we symbolically realize the energy with a cauldron, in which all the other Elements are mixed and transformed, by the color black of the undifferentiated void or the whiteness of the colors all returned and blended. Light is the archetypal symbol for Essence because it allows us to see (to become conscious) and because it radiates equally in all directions (uniting all it touches). When people have spiritual experiences, they are often said to have become "enlightened."

"God is an intelligible sphere— a sphere known to the mind, not to the senses—whose center is everywhere and whose circumference is nowhere."

—Joseph Campbell, *The Power of Myth*

Among many cultures, the symbol for Essence and the symbol for the sun are the same: a circle with a dot in the center. Sometimes Essence is represented solely by the dot, the *bindu*, which is the point of origin and return. Alternatively, Essence may be depicted by the circle, the perfect symbol for wholeness and unity.

Finding a way to symbolize the Elements in a ritual is important. We have given you some general and universal correspondences for them. You will want to express other things in symbolic form in your rituals as well. J. E. Cirlot's *A Dictionary of Symbols* (Philosophical Library, 1962) is a good place to look for ideas. You will also benefit by knowing how to recognize or create symbols that have particular meaning for you.

PERSONALIZING SYMBOLS

You, your life, and your needs are unique. At the same time that you are different and distinctive, due largely to the total of your experiences and how they have affected you, those very experiences may in many ways be common to others. Think of your family of origin—over the years you have found certain similarities with them and certain important differences.

You may have retained the values and meanings of some of your family's symbols, but you may have found things that have particular significance for you—a genre of music, a style of dress, the writing of a certain author, something you like to collect, being around water. Things that have special meaning for you become part of your personal symbology.

We knew a woman who was very involved with her home. To her, home was a sanctuary. She felt that her dwelling and her innermost Self were reflections of each other that had reciprocal influence. When she felt confusion in her life, she put her home in order. Fortunately, she lived in a studio apartment, as she systematically cleaned and straightened everything around, from cupboard to closet. On completion of her ritual task, she sat back and basked in the beauty and order of it all and felt that she had regained a sense of balance. She used her personal symbology and also archetypal symbology, for the home is usually considered a representation of the Self. The cleaning and straightening were cleansing on a symbolic level. The intensity of her involvement brought a sense of inspiration, and relaxing in the center of her ordered space allowed integration, equilibrium, and harmony.

With practice, you can learn to recognize the things in your life that impact you most, that you use symbolically, or with which you identify. And these can be translated into your ritual signature.

ELEMENT SELECTION GUIDE

To assist you in choosing appropriate Elemental symbols for your rituals, use the following tables, which contain possible actions, objects, colors, and sounds for each of the Elements. You will undoubtedly find more symbols to add to these lists. Let these tables be a starting point for your exploration into how the Elements take part in your life.

EARTH ▽

OBJECTS

* Solid, sturdy objects or shapes, such as cubes, globes, or squares

* Stones, metals, crystals, or wood

* Foods: breads, grains, meat, fruits, mushrooms, and other heartyfoods

* Clothing: coats, capes, or other warm, heavy clothes; rough, mottled textures, such as wool

* Scents: heavy, musky odors; the smell of earth, a forest floor, or baking bread

ACTIONS

* Stillness, or slow, steady, deliberate motions

* Lying, sitting, or squatting

* The motions of digging, planting, and harvesting

* Eating—ingestion and digestion

* Moving to each of the four quadrants in your ritual circle

COLORS

* Earth tones: browns, blacks, russets, olive greens, and yellows

* Darkness or a dim, steady light

* Nighttime

SOUNDS

* Silence or the pauses between sounds

* Low, deep tones; slow, steady rhythms

* Bass instruments, such as a drum, fiddle, oboe, or tuba

* Speech that refers to the body, the world, or actions

WATER ▽

OBJECTS

* Water itself and other liquids

* Cups and other liquid containers; crescent shapes

* Seashells, starfish, images of fish, dolphins, and other water inhabitants

* Foods: libations and clear broths

* Clothing: smooth, flowing textures or materials such as silk

* Scents: rain, sea air, or water lilies

ACTIONS

* Fluid, graceful, rhythmic motions

* Actions that denote the giving and receiving aspects of water: pouring, drinking, and washing

* Dancing and swaying

COLORS

* Blues, blue-greens, or silvers

* Filtered or indirect light, gently changing

* Twilight

SOUNDS

* Melodious, flowing sounds

* Rhythmic chanting, rushing water, waves, or rain

* Vibraphone, harp, rhythm section, or alto pitch

* Poetry or singing; speech that appeals to the emotions

Air △

OBJECTS

* Air and wind; round shapes

* Feathers, fans, incense, pin-wheels, books, and pens

* Foods: light desserts such as puff pastry; champagne and other sparkling drinks

* Clothing: light and free-fitting

* Scents: clear and delicate

ACTIONS

* Quick, light motions

* Lifting up or offering up

* Speaking or reading

COLORS

* Sky blue, blues, and whites

* Bright but indirect light, increasing in intensity; electric lighting

* The morning sun

SOUNDS

* Sound itself

* Clear, high-pitched tones; rapid, precise, light rhythms

* The rushing wind, rustling sounds

* Wind chimes, flutes and wood-winds, rattles, bells, or drums

* Speech and laughter; words that direct the thoughts; appeals to reason and logic

Fire △

OBJECTS

* Fire, flame, candles, lamps and fireplaces, torches, matches, sparklers and fireworks; triangular shapes

* Foods: seasoned with hot spices such as cayenne, salsa, Tabasco, or curry; hot foods and drinks

* Clothing: light and warm

* Scents: sharp, tangy smells such as cinnamon; odors from a fire

ACTIONS

* Darting, rapid movements

* Lighting a fire or a candle; burning or sacrificing something

COLORS

* Reds, oranges, and yellows

* Bright, direct, steady light, such as the noontime sun, or a flickering fire, or candlelight

SOUNDS

* Arpeggios and staccato rhythms

* The crackling of a fire, violins and other high-pitched strings, soprano instruments

* Enflaming speeches, stating the intention, invocations, and appeals to Spirit

ESSENCE ☉

OBJECTS

* Central altar, candle, lantern, or lamp
* The ritual circle

ACTIONS

* Standing in the center of the circle
* Holding hands in a circle

COLORS

* Brightness; light itself

SOUNDS

* Sounds of pitch higher than human hearing
* A solitary clear soprano note, a choir's single voice
* Instruments with a lingering echo, such as that which Tibetan bells produce
* In speech, giving thanks for what has been received from Spirit during the invocation

Earth, Water, Air, Fire, and Essence: think of them as basic building blocks, with the earthly physical qualities, watery emotional tendencies, airy mental configurations, fiery bursts of inspirations, and unifying wholism of Essence as their fundamental expressions. The self-exploration questions that follow can help you use the Elements to bring balance to your life.

SELF EXPLORATION

Reflect on the following questions to tune in to how the various Elements play a role in your life. Use your journal to record your insights.

1. With which of the four Elements do you connect the most? the least?

2. Look around your home, your room, or your place of work—the areas that most accurately reflect who you are. Which Elements do you notice? Which ones are missing?

3. Which Elemental influences would help you in your current transition? List the ways you can increase the presence of this Element in your life.

4. Choose a symbol for that Element and symbols for the other three Elements. Place them in a room in the proper quadrants: Air in the Eastern Quadrant, Fire in the Southern Quadrant, Water in the Western Quadrant, and Earth in the Northern Quadrant.

5. Do this exercise to become more grounded and balanced: Each day, stand in the middle of the room, facing east. Be aware you are in the Center and that you connect the grounding energy of Earth with the inspiring energy of sky.

   Focus your attention on the Air symbol, and ask that your thoughts and speech be clear, direct, and lucid for the day.

   Turn to the south, and focus on your Fire symbol. Ask that your creativity, soul, and passion burn clearly and empower you in positive ways.

Turn to the west, and focus on your Water symbol. Ask that you experience your emotions deeply and fully, and express them appropriately.

Turn to the north, and focus on your Earth symbol. Ask that your actions be strong, effective, and right.

Turn back to the east, and focus your attention on Center. Ask that your balance and wholeness may in turn help center and heal others.

Write down your experiences each day.

At the end of the week, read over your journal entries. Write down what you learned and anything new you notice from reading through your experiences this week.

CHAPTER 6

crafting and consecrating tools

While you consider how you wish to bring each of the Elements into your ritual and what symbols represent you, your needs, and your goals, it is important to recall one of the keys to achieving power through ritual expression: the ordinary is replaced by the extraordinary. Let's compare the creation of the extraordinary in a ritual with the transformation of the common to the magical in a theatrical production.

For the first script reading, the actors and actresses sit in chairs and recite their lines. A set designer creates a ground plan for the staging, and in the subsequent script readings, the blocking is done. This is where the actors' places are literally blocked out. The theater company gradually adds props and progressively builds the set. At each of these stages, we can find the magic of creativity, but the transformation to another reality is yet to come. What we are looking for may be experienced during the dress rehearsal, but not until the night of the first performance, the night everyone has been working toward, with costumes and makeup, with the set, music, and lighting flawless, and with the audience waiting in anticipation on the other side of the curtain, does the shift occur. The curtain rises, and everyone succumbs to the spell and enters another world.

"The only domain where the divine is visible is that of art, whatever name we choose to call it."

—André Malraux,
Les Métamorphoses des Dieux

For the theater company, each step is more evocative. An actor becomes involved with a role not only through immersion in the words and gestures of the character, but through every step of the process. When at last the actor dons the makeup and costume, the transformation is complete. The actor steps into the role, and as that being, he or she steps into the reality of the character. Until that time a wig is nothing more than an artificial hairpiece, a drawing room only a stage set.

The tools used in a ritual are just props until they are changed into vehicles for transformation. A stick is not a wand, a table is not an altar, a glass of wine is not a chalice of nectar until you make them so. Your tools can likewise become power objects. They achieve this alchemy by carrying the energy of your intention, being specially crafted and/or consecrated, and by being cared for as if they were symbols of the sacred. You can make or find a tool. When you craft a tool, which may also be called a fetish or talisman, it holds the essence of what it is made from, the essence of who fashions it, and the essence of what it represents.

When a tool becomes a symbol of power, you may want to use it in most or all of your rituals. A power object that represents some important aspect of yourself or your growth can serve as a catalyst to connect you with that energy. You might choose to intensify this connection by creating a kind of permanent altar (a spot on a mantel or shelf) to set up the things that have particular meaning. That way you can have a brief personal ritual just by lighting a candle and being with the energy of the items on your altar.

Power objects are a natural lead-in to rituals. Even the acquisition of these items can be a ritual or ritual-like. You might already have certain things that would appropriately symbolize the different Elements.

A leisurely day at a secluded beach may have yielded a collection of shells, rocks, driftwood, and feathers. You carried these things home and found a way to display them. Looking at them or holding them brings you back to that day, including your thoughts and feelings about it. These treasures already have the power of being able to elicit those pleasant memories; as vehicles capable of bringing on a shift in awareness, they are good options for ritual tools. Use these things alone as they are or creatively combine them to symbolize the mingling of Water, Earth, and Air.

CRAFTING TOOLS

Bring forth more power from these objects by crafting them into fetishes that combine other compatible things that hold the meaning of each Element for you. Here's an example: As I sit here writing this chapter, I find my thoughts are cloudy and lack focus. I decide to make a power object to assist in the unfettered flow of ideas whose goal expresses a particular concept. I decide to make something that ties together Air and Earth. The gift of feathers from a friend's macaw represents Air, I will use red linen thread (red for Fire) for binding, and I will model a bird at rest out of bread dough. Bread exemplifies Earth. I will poke holes in the dough to fit the thread through. When the bird is baked and dry, I will paint it blue for clarity. I will wrap four groups of feathers, three feathers each, into bundles. In numerology, four is the number of the square and Earth, and three is the number of giving form to creative expression. In binding the feathers with the thread, I will bind in the intention with each wrap. Then I will tie each cluster to the bird. After blessing the fetish, I will place it above my desk.

BREAD SCULPTURE DOUGH

4 cups flour

1 cup salt

1 1/2 cups water

Mix and knead the ingredients, adding more water if necessary. After shaping, bake at 300 degrees Fahrenheit for one hour. Paint and shellac.

A power object can have a special purpose, or it may hold the function of a ritual tool that you use repeatedly. If your rituals are likely to include a central altar or four directional altars, you may want to have permanent ritual tools to represent each Element. Use these tools for invoking (calling forth) the energy described by each Element or for evoking the energy (calling it from within). Some of the more commonly used symbols lead the tarot suits: cups or chalices represent Water, discs or pentacles are Earth, knives or swords represent Air, and wands express the energy of Fire. These things can be bought or in some way fashioned, cleansed, and blessed.

The Element Selection Guide at the end of Chapter 5: The Elements of Ritual can give you some ideas of objects, actions, colors, and sounds that exemplify each Element. Certain things may "speak" to you, and these are the things you should consider for your tools. The intention for a ritual might give you ideas about power objects you would like to bring to that ceremony in addition to the Elemental tools. Making power objects may remind you of the projects you created in your first years of school. And indeed, the ideas and instructions for crafts in children's magazines and books are very suitable for this purpose.

Many of the items children use for art projects are just what you need. Construction paper, chalk, paint, beads, buttons, seeds, oatmeal boxes, spools—the list should start unreeling from your early memory by now—will all be useful. Let's start with the materials for masks. A mask is a compelling vehicle for transformation. Make one simply with paper bags, paper plates, or construction paper. The way you will use the mask should partially determine its composition.

Make a mask that is to represent a part of you that you wish to release or transform, such as your anger or fear, from paper so you can burn, tear, bury, or soak it. However, if you want your mask to connect you with the expression of an energy larger than yourself, make it more substantial and elaborate. Decorate a plaster mask with paint, beads, feathers, sequins—almost anything that you can glue on. Several kinds of plaster masks exist, but the following is quite easy and lots of fun.

MAKING A PLASTER MASK

Medical supply stores carry rolls of fast-setting plaster bandages. Buy several rolls to be sure you have enough. You also need a place to lie down, some newspaper or towels to protect the floor and your clothing, a basin of warm water, scissors, a jar of petroleum jelly, and a friend.

1. Pull back your hair, and cover your face with a thin layer of petroleumjelly.

2. Cut the bandage into strips about one inch wide and three inches long.

3. Lie on your back, and have your friend dip the plaster strips into the water, press out any excess water, and then place the strips on your face, making a circle from hairline to ears. Don't go over your nostrils or too far under your chin. You can have any size or shape eye openings and mouth opening, or if you prefer, your eyes and mouth can be closed and covered. The bandages should be built about four layers thick, especially around the edges.

4. After a few minutes, you will feel the first layers hardening and shrinking. When your friend finishes, give the bandages a few minutes more to harden sufficiently.

5. Then, by wiggling your face, the mask will come loose. After you remove the mask, build up any areas you like with extra strips.

6. Let the mask dry thoroughly before you attempt to decorate it.

When one puts on a mask, not only does a transformation of outward appearance occur, but on a more profound level, one's personality or character actually seems to change as well. A kind of metamorphosis occurs in which the inner, often unconscious, or archetypal elements of one's nature are brought forth and allowed expression.

The archetypes have many forms. It's almost as if your inner world were peopled with many different and sometimes incompatible figures. When you hold center stage, you may find yourself uncontrollably acting like an unruly child or a challenged warrior. At other times, you may express the seeker or the wise old one. Many ways besides mask-making exist to work with the archetypes in ritual. In most religions altars with statues represent some form of the Great Spirit.

Create an image of a god or goddess, a power animal, or some aspect of your Self. Mold, paint, and dress a wire figure to achieve a good likeness.

MAKING WIRE FIGURES

14-gauge wire	acrylic or oil paints
steel wool	paintbrush
picture wire	pliers
1 package of papier-mâché mix	wire cutter

1. Twist, cut, and wrap the 14-gauge wire into the skeletal form of the image you choose to create.

2. Use the steel wool to create a musculature, and bind it to the skeleton with the picture wire.

3. Mix the papier-mâché to the consistency of modeling clay, and cover the steel wool with it. Mold or sculpt it for detailing.

4. When the mâché dries, you can paint it. Make garments with paper or cloth and some glue. When you create a figure that comes from your unconscious, don't be surprised if the creation takes on a life of its own.

We can access and channel the energy of our unconscious in other, equally effective ways. One of these is through dreams. Dreamwork, a ritualized way of communicating in the symbolic language of the unconscious, has been practiced from ancient through modern times. Dreams have many levels of expression. The mythic motif connects us with the collective unconscious. Our personal symbols provide doorways into the individual unconscious. Figures and scenes from waking reality can also be seen as symbols that mirror what is likewise a part of our inner world. As the Senoi people of Malaysia use their dreams to guide them in their outer lives, so can we learn to understand and rely on the wisdom of our dreams.

Some dreams have enough impact to provide the outline for a ritual. You can bring figures or symbols from your dreams into ritual as your personal gifts. Not everyone recalls their dreams at first. Recording dreams and impressions from the night when you wake up each morning helps in dream recall. A ritualized means to assist in remembering your dreams is by using a dream pillow. One of the properties of the herb mugwort is to aid in dream recall. Drink a cup of tea made from mugwort before bed each night, or make a small pillow and fill it with the dried herb.

MAKING DREAM PILLOWS

To make a pillow, you need a piece of material about twelve inches long and six inches wide. Choose a color that you associate with night and dreaming. Black and silver are good choices. Collect things for decorations such as crystals, moon shapes, ribbons, beads, or things symbolizing the kinds of dreams you'd like to have. You need an ounce or two of dried mugwort and any aromatic herbs you'd like. If you wish to find insight into your relationship issues, add dried rose petals or buds. Add martial herbs such as ginger or nettle if you are looking for dreams to speak of your assertiveness or aggressiveness.

1. Bind, glue, or stitch any decorations onto the outside of the material.

2. Fold it in half inside out, and sew up the sides and most of the top, leaving a hole about an inch and a half wide at the corner.

3. Turn the bag to the right side through the hole and fill the bag with the herbs.

4. Stitch the hole shut.

After blessing and consecrating the bag, place it on your pillow. Before you go to sleep each night, hold the bag for a few minutes while you meditate on remembering your dreams. Sleep with the bag near your head.

MAKING HERBAL INCENSE

Dried herbs are known to have medicinal properties. Chamomile is relaxing and soothing. Peppermint soothes your stomach as well as clears your head. Take herbs internally or use them in other ways. Herbs, roots, gums, oils, and resins are used in making incense. Make your own by mixing the dried ingredients with a mortar and pestle and moistening them very slightly with oil. As you grind, mentally add the intention you wish the incense smoke to carry. Much easier than making your own incense is buying a roll of charcoals and burning the herbs and flowers on one of the discs.

The smoke from the burning incense bestows a cleansing or healing as it fills the air around you and within you. A change must occur on both an inner and an outer level for healing to occur. Sometimes change takes place within and is grounded through outward expression; other times the outer resonates inward. This is one of the reasons we use the act of eating in ritual. It is a way to take something in symbolically and make it a part of you. When the incorporation of some quality is the purpose of your ritual, enhance this by modeling a power object representing that state out of something edible. A sweet choice is marzipan.

MODELING MARZIPAN

Make marzipan by mixing ground almonds, egg white, and sugar, or purchase a tube of almond paste and follow the recipe on the label. Add food coloring if you like. Mold or sculpt any object you wish, or make a bowl to hold other ritual foods. When the piece dries, glaze it with diluted egg white.

It seems that candles have a place in every ritual. If you make them yourself, they have even more meaning. Sand candles are easily molded in a bucket of tightly packed damp sand.

MAKING SAND CANDLES

large pot of water

canning wax

an old can (must fit inside the pot of water)

crayons

clean paint stick

deep tub or box filled with 5 to 6 inches of clean sand

small, round bowl

candle wicking

paperclip or candle wick bottom

pencil to hold up the wick

1. Place the pot of water over low heat. Put the canning wax in the old can and set this in the pot of water (like a double boiler) to melt the wax.

2. When the canning wax has melted, break the crayons into small pieces and place them in the wax to melt. Stir gently with the paint stick to distribute the crayon color.

3. Dampen the sand in the tub so it will hold a shape. Use the bowl to make a depression in the sand, then use your finger to make some "legs" for the bowl depression.

4. Cut a piece of candle wicking equal in length to the depth of the bowl plus approximately 3 inches. Secure one end of the wick to the paperclip and tie the other end to the pencil. Bury the wick in the sand in the middle of the sand bowl and lie the pencil across the top of the sand bowl.

5. Carefully pour the melted wax into the sand bowl, making sure the wick is straight. Let the wax cool until the wick no longer moves within the wax.

6. When the candle has completely hardened, dig it up out of the sand. Wipe off the excess sand and enjoy.

Of course, sand candles are not suitable for all ritual purposes. You might find dipped candles to have a wider range of uses.

MAKING DIPPED CANDLES

large, deep pot of water

canning wax

a deep can (must fit inside the pot of water)

crayons

clean paint stick

long piece of candle wicking

pencil to hold up the wick

1. Place the pot of water over low heat. Put the canning wax in the old can and set this in the pot of water (like a double boiler) to melt the wax.

2. When the canning wax has melted, break the crayons into small pieces and place them in the wax to melt. Stir gently with the paint stick to distribute the crayon color.

3. Fasten one end of the wick to a pencil, and dip the free end of the wick into the wax. Take it out, let it harden, and then dip it again.

> 4. Repeat this procedure until the candle is as fat as you want it. You may need to reheat the wax from time to time.
>
> **Dipped candles are often made in pairs, one wick dipped at both ends. When the candles dry, they can be carved.**

You may use candles to symbolize illumination, but you can also represent light or clarity in other ways. Many of you may remember the wicked stepmother in the story of Snow White. Each day she gazed into her magic looking glass and chanted, "Looking-glass upon the wall, who is fairest of us all?" And the mirror would reply.

Mirrors symbolize truth, the reflection of divine wisdom. In rituals, use them to scry. When one mentally holds a question while gazing intently and single-mindedly into water, a crystal ball, or a mirror, a powerful form of symbol immersion takes place. This concentrated involvement with a symbol can unleash its many meanings.

As a ritual object, a mirror has the power of representing all of the Elements: Air △ , vision; Fire △ , insight and illumination; Essence ☉ , seeing, as in coming to consciousness; Water ▽ , reflection; and Earth ▽ , the vehicle that contains these qualities. Betty Edwards, in *Drawing on the Artist Within* (Simon & Schuster, 1986), explores the concepts of illumination, intuition, and insight. She states:

> The root of **intuition** is **intuitus**. . .[from] the Latin verb **intueri,** to look at, and the word is defined as "the power or faculty of attaining direct knowledge or cognition without rational thought and inferences"—seeing

*something directly, or, in other words, "getting the picture," without having to figure it out…. A partner to intuition, **insight,** paradoxically refers directly to seeing and vision but means seeing something not necessarily visible, such as "seeing into" something, or "apprehending" something.*

MAKING A MAGIC MIRROR

Make a magic mirror simply by gluing black felt to the back of a hand mirror, consecrating the mirror, and keeping it wrapped in black silk.

CONSECRATION

Now that you have some ideas about how to make power objects to use in your rituals, you're ready to move on to the next stage of tool preparation—consecration. To consecrate a tool means to make it sacred. Some of the objects you choose to use in your rituals may already be sacred. A spiritual or religious statue or icon kept in a place of honor can certainly be an expression of the sacred. Yet you may find that the process of cleansing it allows its inherent quality to be even more present.

A complete cleansing involves the use of all five Elements, although one can perform very effective work using the expression of a single Element. I remember being mystified as a child when my mother would ceremoniously bury something in the backyard to cleanse it. In my mind there was no way something would become clean by lying in the dirt for two weeks. Unfortunately, my mother was unfamiliar with the principles underlying her actions. She could not explain that by burying something in the earth, or returning it to the Mother, it was neutralized and reborn as if new.

In a five-Element cleansing, use Earth, preferably the purified type that is sold as potting soil, or salt crystals. For the Element of Water, use boiled or bottled water. Air cleansings are commonly done by smudging, the passing of burning incense or herbs. To cleanse with Fire means to pass the object through a flame, or for things for which this would not be suitable, touch a rose to them instead. The Element of Essence is most easily represented by the sun.

Ideally, you should first cleanse every Elemental representation by Essence. This means putting the salt, incense, and rose or candle on separate plates (preferably glass), the water in a carafe, and then placing all of these things in a safe, somewhat secluded spot where they can bathe in the sun's light. Ask that the rays of the sun purify these things as Essential energy envelops them.

After a few hours, remove the Elemental tools from the sunlight. Take the plate of salt, touch your hand to it, and state, "May this salt be blessed with love and light. May all things negative be gone, and may only that which is good be held within." Do the appropriate version of the same blessing for each of the other Elemental objects. When you finish, the Elemental symbols are ready to use in a ritual or to consecrate your tools.

For consecration, sprinkle your tools with water, sprinkle with or touch them to salt, pass them through the flame of the candle or touch them with the rose, encircle them with the smoke of the burning incense, and hold them up toward the sun. This process is similar to the consecration done during a ritual. When you create the ritual space, perform the cleansing by walking around the space with the burning incense and then the lit candle, sprinkling the space with a mixture of the salt and the water, and imagining the sun filling and surrounding the area. When you circle the space with the Elements, it is good to walk sunwise (clockwise), which creates energy. Counterclockwise movements break energy down.

Perform the same process for each of the ritual participants, as well as for the altar items. In doing consecrations, the cleansing may be all or just part of the procedure. A blessing can be included with the cleansing to fill the ritual space, objects, and members with their own Essential energy, after cleansing them of whatever was interfering or outmoded. Some blessings have the cleansing built in, and some cleansings include a blessing.

A blessing is a gift from the heart. Adapt songs, poems, or chants that touch your heart to your needs. Joan Halifax, Ph.D., Buddhist teacher and anthropologist, taught me a Native American chant that makes a beautiful blessing: "Oh, Great Spirit, Earth, Sun, Sky, and Sea: You are inside and all around me." As you speak or sing this chant, visualizing its message provides the blessing and cleansing.

Visualization is an excellent form of cleansing. Using color energy, imagine a clear cloud or beam of the color passing through yourself or your tools. The color washes away whatever needs to be cleansed. Then imagine that the chosen color remains, filling and surrounding you or your tools with its energy. The box shows some traditional meanings associated with the colors. You may wish to "try on" various colors to discover what feelings they evoke for you.

Charge a glass of water by mentally filling it with a color. Then use the water for dipping, sprinkling, or drinking. Another way to charge water is by making a sun tea with stones. Sun teas are generally herbs placed into a jar of water and left in the sun. Stones and gemstones have healing properties as well. Use emeralds for directing passions, rose quartz to bring peace to your heart, amethyst for balance and forgiveness, and opals to improve intuition. Lapidary shops sell not only the stones, but books explaining the correspondences.

You can find most of the items in this chapter at craft shops, art supply stores, medical suppliers, or in nature. Never let the lack of the exact ingredient prevent you from making a tool. Even use the things you have around the house if you properly cleanse them and then treat them as if they were no longer ordinary objects.

COLOR CHART

Black—silence and the mysteries

Brown—the earth; solidity, stability

Purple—religious dogma

Lavender—spiritual energy

Navy blue—institutionalized thought

Sky blue—clarity

Turquoise blue—insight

Green—growth

Yellow—warmth

Orange—vitality

Red—passion

Silver—lunar power

Gold—solar power

White—safety, protection

SELF EXPLORATION

Reflect on the following questions to learn what objects might become tools for ritual use. Record your discoveries in your journal.

1. What power objects do you have now or have you had in the past? What made them powerful? What do they symbolize for you?

   Were these objects special in themselves, or did you, another person, or an event imbue them with this special energy?

2. Have you ever intentionally charged an object with a particular energy? How? Which steps listed in this chapter did you use?

3. After reading this chapter, what ritual tool are you inspired to make or bless to help you with your current transition? With what particular energy do you want to charge it?

4. Write out your plan for creating and blessing this tool.

5. After you complete your ritual tool, place it in the appropriate direction quadrant and use it in your morning ritual. Write down your experiences.

At the end of the week, read over your journal entries. Write down what you learned and anything new you notice from reading through your experiences this week.

CHAPTER 7

altars

An altar provides a symbol of the integrated wholeness of the Self and of the universe. It is the pivotal center point of balanced energies for your circle, for your consciousness. The word *altar* derives from the Latin *altare*, "a high place," and the use of high grounds as places of worship has been common to many cultures throughout human history.

Elevation allows you to see your surroundings; given the right weather, standing on high ground allows you to see the circle of the horizon around you as the central point—the image of Spirit. High places also allow clearer access to viewing the heavens, to metaphorically entering other worlds or planes of consciousness, and to receiving the guiding light of Spirit from the stars above.

A person standing atop a high place becomes a central pillar, mediating between the earth and the heavens, the interface between Spirit and matter, an *axis mundi*, which conducts energies between the planes of existence. Standing at the center is also symbolic of the birth of the universe, the One point manifesting from the zero, the line manifesting from the point.

Creating an altar is, in essence, recreating the origin of existence, and each time you construct or change an altar you have access to reliving this vital myth.

"We must never forget that one of the essential functions of the myth is its provision of an opening into the Great Time, a periodic re-entry into Time primordial."

—Mircea Eliade,
Myths, Dreams, and Mysteries

MAKING AN ALTAR

Different cultures have different types of altars. Some people use high ground, some construct a mound of earth for an altar, while others spend much time and energy on ornate altars built to precise specifications. All altars have some common symbolism, which you can use in making your altars.

HEIGHT

As discussed above, elevation is important in symbolically raising consciousness to the level of the sacred. However, the height does not need to be extreme. In your home, a small table, windowsill, or shelf is fine. A mantelpiece not only has extra height, but also carries the symbolism of the inner fire of Spirit in the fireplace below.

ALTAR SURFACE OR ALTAR CLOTH

The surface of your altar represents the emergence of something out of nothing in the reenactment of the origination myth. When you begin to set up an altar, after allowing the elevation of the altar itself to raise your consciousness, imagine the top of the altar, or the placing of the altar cloth, to represent the emergence from the Void of a sense of limitlessness. View the altar surface as a kind of infinite canvas on which Spirit creates its manifestations.

THE CENTER

From this endless expanse of possibility arises a point in the Center, from which all else emanates. This point is the One that contains all, the One in which everything finds relationship and meaning. On your altar, you may represent this One by the altar cloth, by a simple symbol in the center of the altar, or by a central white candle or a plain oil lamp. The candle or lamp holds the special meaning of the light of Spirit or Essence, the one unifying light, as well as the sense of the *axis mundi*, which signifies our striving toward balance between Spirit and matter.

THE ELEMENTS

As the One has risen from limitless possibility, so do the four qualities of the Elements arise from the One. As you build your altar, you recreate this primal myth of emergence, and as you place your Elemental symbols on the altar, you recreate time and space. Imagine each Elemental tool to issue from the Center, from the One, as you place it in its appropriate quadrant (see Chapter 5: The Elements of Ritual).

TYPES AND USES OF ALTARS

Altars can be simple or complex, temporary or permanent, consistent or changing. Below, find five categories of uses for altars. These categories correspond with Essence and the four Elements.

ESSENCE

To honor and increase your relationship with Spirit, you may choose to design a simple altar, which includes elevation, the altar surface or an altar cloth, and a single candle as described earlier. If you tend to the altar daily, you symbolically attend to the sacred in yourself and in your world. Taking a moment on rising in the morning to light the candle—striking the match high in the air and bringing it down to the wick is a gesture that represents bringing the higher energies of Spirit into the world—and imagining the light filling you is a fine way to center yourself in Spirit for the day.

INITIATION/ENERGY

You may want to honor specific aspects of the sacred in yourself and in your life. An altar that includes the four Elements as well as Essence can help balance and align you with these energies. Another way to bring this balance more fully into your life is to make an altar for each Element and set them up in the corresponding directional areas of a room. These altars can be as simple as four different colored candles, or use Elemental tools in each of the quadrants. You can set up any of the altars described here around a room or on a single altar; choose whichever is more useful for you. If you feel you need to expand your consciousness, multiple altars might work better than a single one, whereas a single altar may help increase your focus and concentration.

MERGING/MIND

You can also create altars to manifest certain qualities of the sacred you feel you need. If, for example, you feel you have been too harsh on yourself or others, you might want to build an altar for increasing compassion in yourself.

To accomplish this, you might choose your Elemental symbols from aspects of Water, which can symbolize giving, forgiveness, and an ability to flow around obstacles. You could place a soft blue towel on top of your altar cloth to represent a sea of loving kindness, a fan of

appropriate colors in the east to symbolize gentleness of thought, and a votive
candle in a blue glass candleholder in the
south to represent the softening of too-
hot energies. A delicate vase with blue
and white flowers or a silver cup of water
in the west can remind you to be tender
in your emotions that they may give rise
to beauty, and a seashell in the north can
help you ground your energies in a
pleasing and sound manner.

DEEPENING/FEELING

Honor the cyclical events in your life with
altars. Many people decorate their homes
with seasonal bouquets or other adorn-
ments representative of the time of year.

Consciously constructing an altar to celebrate the season not only brings
beauty to your house, but also helps you deepen your relationship to
nature, your humanity, and Spirit.

A mantelpiece altar to recognize the return of the light during the
winter solstice can use traditional winter symbols to help deepen your
connection to your own inner light. A black, deep green, or burgundy
cloth can represent both the Void from which the One arises and the
darkness of the winter days, which give birth to the light in mid-
December. This light of Spirit can be present in a tall, central oil lamp,
with a candle on each side representing the Element of Fire. Use a black

and a white candle to signify the polarities with which many of us struggle during the dark times of our lives, which the higher light of Spirit brings into proper relationship; or choose to use the traditional colors of red and green. These colors, too, imply a dance toward balance, with the cleansing and burning qualities of Fire always seeking equilibrium with the verdant expansion of natural growth.

Also show this theme of balance and equilibrium by using gray ribbons to represent the smoothing of emotions for the Element of Water, with expression in sound taking form on your altar with jingle bells on the ribbon ends for Air. Use the plants of the season for Earth, holly providing the idea of increasing form with its sharp edges and red berries, and the softer shape of mistletoe, which grows not on the ground but high up in trees, giving rise to the concept of expansion. Creating such an altar can help you align the imbalances in yourself and approach your inner light, as we all approach the returning light at the solstice.

MANIFESTATION/BODY

The altars you create for your rituals can be focal points for raising and stirring the consciousness of the participants. While all rituals contain the Elements, follow the same basic process, and reenact an archetypal myth, each ritual is unique to its particular time, place, and the individuals involved in it. The ritual altar reflects its singularity in your choice of Elemental symbols and their relationships to each other.

Chapter 5: The Elements of Ritual gives you guidelines for personalizing symbols, and we hope that the following altar ideas for each type of ritual help you integrate that information as well as inspire you creatively.

BEGINNINGS

When something new presents itself to you—something you have, do, or become—design a ritual to help you define how this newness fits into your life. The ritual can include your hopes and wishes, protection against your fears, or can simply be a welcoming.

ALTAR FOR A BABY-NAMING RITUAL

Some good friends of ours had their first baby. After much deliberation, they chose to name their baby girl Rose, because it was their flower during courtship and because the rose symbolized perfection, love, and heartfulness. They designed the altar for Rose's naming ritual around the significance of their love and hopes for her and the beauty of the flower for which she was to be named.

For an altar cloth, they used a beautiful baby blanket they received as a gift and adorned it with pink and white ribbons, the colors those

of the baby roses that surrounded the central candle and that symbolized, to them, purity and heart. The central candle was white and
inscribed with Rose's full name, with the intention that as it burned,
their child might be filled with and fueled by the light of Spirit. The
Fire Element was represented on the altar by a stained glass night-light
in the shape of a rose, a gift from another friend who wished the light
of love to shine forth even in the dark times of the new baby's life.
Rose's aunt wrote a calligraphic explanation of the choice and meaning
of Rose's name. They placed this in the eastern quadrant of the altar and
saved it for Rose to read when she was older. In the west was a bowl of
rosewater, which had also been charged with the baby's birthstone, and
a cloth with which to wipe her forehead, hands, and feet during the ritual. For the Element of Earth, the parents acquired a small evergreen
sapling and a trowel to use in planting it in a special spot in their backyard; caring for the tree during Rose's life would remind them of this
ritual and they would symbolically be attending to her soul.

MERGINGS

A merging is the coming together of two or more entities to form something larger than the individuals themselves. A marriage is the ultimate
personal merging, and a wedding may include many powerful symbols.

ALTAR FOR A WEDDING RITUAL

This wedding altar has a white altar cloth topped with ribbons woven
together to symbolize the merging of two separate lives into a new and
larger life, which can bring even more beauty and creation to the world
than each could separately. Black and white candles represent the

receptive and the dynamic, which merge into the light of Spirit while retaining individuality. Place the marriage certificate and bells the couple will use in the ceremony in the east and an entwined candle in the south. In the west place a glass of wine ready to be blessed with the wishes of a few friends and family members and then drunk by the happy couple. The wedding rings occupy the northern area of the altar, to be given in the ritual as a token of the couple's love and commitment.

CYCLES

The celebration of cycles or anniversaries gives our lives continuity. These occasions also help us measure our growth and look toward new possibilities. On the eve of a new year, as we look both back and ahead, we celebrate the inner distance traveled and clarify our goals for the coming year.

A NEW YEAR'S EVE ALTAR

Set up these altars around a room, allowing space for a large number of people to walk from station to station. In the east, the station of Air holds a table with paper and pens for guests to write down those parts of themselves that are antiquated and that hold them back from entering the new year fully attuned to their inner selves and the will of Spirit. Cast these papers on the fire burning in the fireplace in the south, after which the participants can move to the table in the western quadrant of the room, to further cleanse themselves with a drink of champagne or sparkling water. Canapés from the northern table can help them ground their resolutions for the coming year, and all can gather around the candle on the central table, donning party hats and using noisemakers to celebrate the inner and outer return of another year.

ENDINGS

An ending is a form of completion that is often experienced as a loss. When something with which you associate or identify changes in relation to you, it is important to acknowledge what changed and what you gained. A loss is only as important as the relationship that preceded it.

A RITUAL ALTAR FOR LEAVING HOME

When a teenager leaves home for college, it can bring up many varied and often conflicting emotions for the family. An ending ritual can be useful in honoring this major transition. We helped one family, who all got along well, design a ritual similar to the one described for you here. You should personalize the symbols to be appropriate for your family.

Parents and siblings can spend time choosing photographs of precious moments together with the graduate; these pictures embody the spirit of their family. Place them around a candleholder, which occupies the center of the altar. To express their support of continued communication with their daughter, the parents place stamps and a long-distance telephone card in the quadrant for Air. Together the family can selected a garnet pendant or ring for the teenager and place it in the south to represent the energetic family support they desire to send with the graduate on this new life journey. A younger sister can place a gift of a bottle of favorite bubble bath in the west, so the graduate can find emotional comfort in a warm bath and the love of her sister, as her sister has so often found solace in the care of her elder sibling. The younger brother can make fudge, cut it into big cubes, and place them in a box in the north, to let the graduate know he thinks she is sweet and so she can have some nourishment from him on her trip.

After the family gives the gifts to the graduate, she can place her gifts to the family on the altar: in the east, a letter to the family, thanking them for what she has learned and how she has grown from being in a relationship with each family member and with the family as a group; a homemade candle in the south, symbolizing how they helped her find her inner light; a tape of her playing guitar and singing the family's favorite songs in the west; and a ceramic bowl filled with cookies especially baked with love in the north. Spirit is represented in the center of the altar by a picture she painted.

HEALINGS

To heal means to make whole. To heal, you must often embrace and take ownership of the things you would most like to let go; it is important to remember that you cannot let go of things you do not own. Other times, healing may be simply a matter of nurturing.

A Ritual Altar for Rest and Relaxation

Sometimes you may get overworked and overextended; you may have difficulty sleeping or be just plain exhausted. In addition to developing a plan to keep your commitments in reasonable limits, a nightly ritual could help heal your exhaustion.

Set up an altar on your night table to help you release your concerns of the day, center into yourself, and receive the nourishment of Spirit while you sleep. Light an oil lamp in the center of the altar to invoke Spirit, and from that flame, light a stick of your favorite incense to lift away your concerns for the night. Write in your journal while you sip warm milk flavored with vanilla, and gaze at a lovely piece of rose quartz in the light of the lamp before extinguishing the flame and going to sleep.

While you might create an altar to help you with a transition or one that focuses on one of the Elements, you may also find that you spontaneously create altars with no specific goal in mind. These usually begin

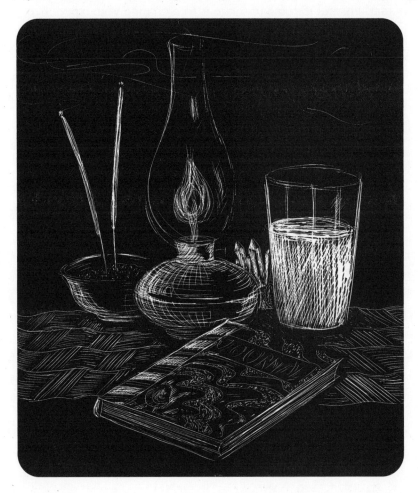

as collections that become more elaborate over time. If you notice a theme emerging on a shelf or windowsill, you might want to bring intention to the space and transform it into a formal altar. This could be particularly useful if you can relate it to a change you experience.

SELF EXPLORATION

Reflect on the following questions to clarify how you can use an altar in your ritual. Use your journal to take notes.

1. What type of altar would assist you in your current transition? What do you want the altar to do for you during this time? What will you use for the body of the altar itself? What will this represent to you?

2. What color altar cloth would best serve your purpose? What material? What will these represent to you?

3. What Elemental symbols and colors will you use? What does each represent?

4. Construct your altar and use it in your morning ritual. Record your experiences, including any changes you make to the altar, why you made them, and the effects of the change on your experience.

At the end of the week, read over your journal entries. Write down what you learned and anything new you notice from reading through your experiences this week.

CHAPTER 8

ritual guidelines and worksheet

In the four previous chapters, you received all the basic information needed to create your own rituals. This chapter assists you in integrating, in a simple manner, the information and techniques from those chapters. By using what you have learned and following the guidelines and worksheet presented here, you should be able to create a balanced, empowering ritual for any occasion.

TEN GUIDELINES FOR CREATING YOUR OWN RITUALS

The guidelines are simple but important. The worksheet corresponds to the steps explained in Chapter 4: The Process of Ritual, and you can use it for each ritual you create.

1. Remember the intention.

2. Let the myth inspire you.

3. Use your intuition.

4. A ritual should benefit all and harm none.

5. Keep it simple.

6. Stay balanced.

7. Keep in touch with your feelings and with the other people.

8. Honor the power of words.

9. Keep the imagination alive.

10. Attend to detail.

REMEMBER THE INTENTION

In both the creation and performance of a ritual, the intention is the guiding force; without its presence, a ritual becomes a shell of what it can be. If at any point in the process—preparation, manifestation, or grounding—you find yourself worried, confused, or aggravated, you have lost touch with the intention. Focus your thoughts on the intention or take a few breaths to release the distractions, and speak the intention silently or aloud until you are back in sync with it.

LET THE MYTH INSPIRE YOU

You do not need to feel that you must formulate or enact a ritual merely on the strengths of your personal mind, desires, and talents. A ritual admits you to sacred time and space, into the archetypal realm of myth and mystery. You might choose to research myths and fairy tales with the same theme as the ritual you are planning or explore how other cultures realize intentions similar to yours. Allow yourself to be touched by our ancestral wisdom and the guidance of Spirit.

Use Your Intuition

Sometimes the inspiration of myth can give you so many ideas you don't know what to do with them. Allow your inner sense of the intention, and of what is appropriate, to help you contain and provide form for your ideas. Imagine what the ritual can be like, and after thinking about what you can do, sit quietly, holding in your mind the plans you have made. Allow yourself to become aware of how this ritual would feel when enacted: Is it right for your purpose? Do you understand the meaning of the Elements you chose, and are they appropriate? Give equal time to intellect and intuition in planning a ritual, and it will be balanced and powerful.

A Ritual Should Benefit All and Harm None

Participation in a ritual allows entry to mythic dimensions, from which we can increase both our consciousness and relatedness to ourselves, one another, our world, and Spirit. Any ritual that bears malice will reduce, if not destroy, the potential for healing that ritual holds. Malice affects not only the person at whom it is aimed, but the person who generates it as well.

Keep It Simple

It is easy to get carried away with the grandeur of myth when formulating rituals. Remember, however, that simple rituals are easier for most people to follow and that focusing on a few symbolic acts provides a better avenue for entry into mythic consciousness than does a ritual cluttered with symbols and stories. The ritual should be short enough to hold the attention of all present, so omit all that you do not really need.

Stay Balanced

As we discussed in Chapter 5: The Elements of Ritual, balancing the actions and objects that represent the different aspects of yourself and the world is important. Throughout the various stages of creating your rituals, keep track of when you get off balance: worrying over details, getting washed over with intense feelings, letting pride interfere with the intention. Allow the balance you create in the ritual to remind you of the center in yourself, and allow your inner balance to flow into the ritual. Following the rhythms of your breath and attending to the intention are two simple ways of returning to your center.

Keep in Touch with Your Feelings and with the Other People

Increasing relationship is an important function of ritual, and so throughout the process, attend to your feelings about yourself, the work, and the quality of connection among the participants. The more easily and smoothly you communicate feelings and ideas during the preparation stage, the more you and the others will be open to the power and motion of the ritual in manifestation.

Honor the Power of Words

What is spoken during a ritual has a much greater impact than if spoken in normal space-time. Because of this, choose what to say and how to express it with great care. While it is fine for some rituals to provide space for participants to speak from their hearts, for the most part, little extemporaneous speaking should occur. Select poems or write words that mean exactly what you wish to convey, and practice delivering them for the best possible effect.

Keep the Imagination Alive

We enter myth through the vitality of imagination. The symbology of a ritual should be a means to tap into the participants' unconscious. The simplicity of a ritual should allow their imaginations to create the consciousness of the myth that you are enacting. An easily recognizable vibrancy and regeneration occur when this consciousness is present.

Attend to Detail

Every object and action in a ritual is there to help us alter consciousness in a specific way that honors the intention of the ritual. If you attend to the details, the impact of the ritual will be much greater, as you will bring the quality of the sacred into each particular aspect of the work. Rehearsals are of great benefit in helping you set the proper tone, regulating the timing of actions, and reducing performance anxiety so that your attention during the ritual itself can focus on the ritual intention. Even if a full rehearsal is not possible, practicing your actions and what you will say helps. Everything you do in a ritual has symbolic meaning and impact, so attend to the details.

Chapter 4: The Process of Ritual led you through the planning, manifesting, and grounding of a ritual. The following Ritual Worksheet expands on the Process Planning Guide, integrates the information on Elements and symbol selection from Chapter 5: The Elements of Ritual, and provides you with space to write in all the details needed at each stage of your ritual.

To help you better understand how a ritual works, each stage and each section is marked with its Elemental symbol: $\triangle$ Fire, $\triangle$ Air, ∇ Water,

▽ Earth, or ⊙ Essence. For a ritual to have symmetry, it follows the stages of inspiration △, creation △, formation or deepening ▽, and action or manifestation ▽, as does any creative process. In astronomical theory, the stars were born from the condensation of the primal, or "essential" matter of the universe. The fiery masses that are stars produced gases that as they cooled, further condensed into liquids and then solids. Looking at this process in terms of the Elements, we see that Essence gives rise to Fire, from which issue increasingly "denser" manifestations of being: Air to Water to Earth. These stages of the development of the universe are analogous to those of a ritual.

In each of these stages, the four Elements are also present in energy △, mind △, feeling ▽, and objects or actions ▽. We discussed these stages and Elements in the previous two chapters. By using this worksheet, you will gain a better understanding of their relationships to each other and of their interactions in a ritual.

In the preparation stage, notice that the stages flow downward from inspiration to action into the beginning stages of the manifestation of the ritual. There the movement progresses from Earth back up toward Fire and Essence, at the invocation and direction of higher energies. These energies are then brought down through the Elements from Fire to Earth again in the closure of the ritual. The grounding phase again brings the flow from Earth to Fire, making a complete round of the Elements—from Fire (inspiration for the ritual) to Earth (physical preparation creating sacred space) to Fire (invocation) to Earth (ritual closure/breakdown of sacred space) to Fire (integration). The central point of this cycle is Spirit or Essence, and the beginning and the ending are inspiration. So, too, is it with existence (find a basic outline of this process in Chapter 10: Conclusion).

While you may not need to use the worksheet for simple rituals, you may find it essential in organizing more complex ones. We recommend working with it a few times until you integrate all aspects of creating rituals and feel comfortable without the worksheet. Even then, it can serve as a useful guideline.

RITUAL WORKSHEET

PREPARATION/CREATION

△ **Clarifying the Intention (Inspiration)**

△ 1. What is the inspiration for this ritual?

_____

_____

_____

△ 2. What myth does it reenact? What type of ritual is it?

_____

_____

_____

▽ 3. What effect do you want this ritual to have, and on whom?

_____

_____

_____

▽ 4. Clearly state the intention of this ritual:

_____

_____

_____

△ Planning (Creation)

△ 1. What symbols will you use in this ritual?

Fire _____

Air _____

Water _____

Earth _____

Essence _____

△ 2. Write out a draft of the ritual itself, following the steps described in Chapter 4: The Process of Ritual and the Manifestation section below for guides.

_____

_____

_____

▽ 3. Logistics: Write out dates, times, deadlines, what needs coordination, and who you need to contact.

_____

_____

_____

▽ 4. Make a shopping list of materials you need.

_____

_____

_____

▽ Emotional Processing (Deepening)

△ 1. What feelings or issues have the preparations you've done so far brought up?

_____

_____

_____

△ 2. Have any ethical questions arisen? Is there any way this ritual could hold negative intention for anyone? How?

_____

_____

_____

▽ 3. What other limitations (money, space, time) have you encountered?

_____

_____

_____

▽ 4. Working through these feelings, ethical issues, and limitations, what adjustments, if any, do you need to make to your ritual plan?

_____

_____

_____

▽ Physical Preparation (Action)

△ 1. What else do you need to coordinate?

_____

_____

_____

△ 2. What materials do you need to gather?

_____

_____

_____

▽ 3. Leave details for arriving with helpers, and check that you have everything you need.

_____

_____

_____

▽ 4. Cleaning the physical space: what needs to be done, when, and by whom?

_____

_____

_____

MANIFESTATION: THE RITUAL ITSELF

▽ Creating Sacred Space (Action)

▽ 1. What objects and actions will you use to clear and bless the space?

_____

_____

_____

▽ 2. What emotions do you need to clear from yourself? How will you do this?

_____

_____

_____

△ 3. How will you center yourself?

_____

_____

_____

△ 4. How will you ask for guidance in conducting this ritual?

_____

_____

_____

Using the circle at left, write how you will set up the temple/sacred space, including location of your chosen symbols, where participants will enter and stand, and other appropriate details.

_____

_____

_____

_____

_____

_____

Setting the Mood (Deepening ▽) and Declaration of Intention (Creation △)

▽ 1. What objects and actions will you use?

_____

_____

_____

∇ 2. Music and sounds?

_____

_____

_____

△ 3. Poetry and speech?

_____

_____

_____

△ 4. What will these things inspire in the participants?

_____

_____

_____

⊙ Invocation (Inspiration △) and Direction of Higher Energies (Creation △)

△ 1. What particular energies will you invoke, and precisely what do you want them to do?

_____

_____

_____

△ 2. What words will you use to direct these energies to their purpose?

_____

_____

_____

▽ 3. What emotions will be touched, and what kinds of rhythms or music will help you accomplish this?

_____

_____

_____

▽ 4. What objects and actions will best represent and channel these energies and the emotions of the participants?

_____

_____

_____

Blessing (Deepening ▽) and Closure (Action ▽)

△ 1. With what gift of Spirit will the participants leave the ritual?

_____

_____

_____

△ 2. Words of poetry you can use to name this gift:

_____

_____

_____

_____

▽ 3. Music and sounds to enhance the gift and mark the ending of the ritual:

_____

_____

_____

▽ 4. Actions and objects used to mark the ending: how will the participants leave the sacred space?

_____

_____

_____

GROUNDING/COMPLETION

▽ Breakdown of Sacred Space (Action)

△ 1. What is left to be done (blessed food or drink that needs proper disposal, for example)?

_____

_____

_____

△ 2. How will you release the sacred spaced back to normal space?

_____

_____

_____

▽ 3. Emotional completion: how will you give thanks?

_____

_____

_____

▽ 4. When will you break down the circle, put things away, and clean up? Who will help?

_____

_____

_____

▽ Emotional Process (Deepening)

▽ 1. Did you experience any strong physical sensations during the ritual?

_____

_____

_____

▽ 2. What emotions were raised?

_____

_____

_____

△ 3. What did you learn about yourself?

_____

_____

_____

△ 4. How does your emotional experience relate to the myth enacted in the ritual?

_____

_____

_____

△ Evaluation (Creation)

▽ 1. What did and didn't work effectively?

_____

_____

_____

▽ 2. How much impact did the ritual have on those involved?

_____

_____

_____

△ 3. If you were to do this ritual again, how would you improve it?

_____

_____

_____

△ 4. What new ideas or insights did you gain about the nature of ritual?

_____

_____

_____

△ Integration (Inspiration)

△ 1. How did this ritual inspire you?

_____

_____

_____

△ 2. How can you use this inspiration to create change in yourself?

_____

_____

_____

▽ 3. What form do you imagine these changes can take in the world?

_____

_____

_____

▽ 4. What actions can you take this week to manifest this inspiration?

_____

_____

_____

SELF EXPLORATION

Using the guidelines and worksheets in this chapter, create and perform a ritual to help you in your current transition. Use the process notes in the worksheets, and write down any other notes in your journal.

CHAPTER 9

applications of ritual

Throughout this book, we give you numerous examples of the applications of ritual and help you see where ritual can be useful in your life. This chapter further explores ways ritual can create balance and strength in your life as an individual and as a person in relationship with others.

We have divided this chapter into four sections: Individual Rituals, Rituals in Relationships, Family Rituals, and Group Rituals. In each section, we approach the application of ritual from four different directions: the physical world of manifestation, the emotional world of deepening, the mental world of relatedness, and the spiritual world of initiation. These approaches correspond to the Elements of Earth, Water, Air, and Fire, which we discussed in Chapter 5: The Elements of Ritual and have been a common theme throughout this book. Each section provides examples of rituals that will enable you to recognize and use ritual as a powerful tool in your life.

INDIVIDUAL RITUALS

In addition to using rituals to help cope with change, you can also create rituals to help you make changes.

"Most native societies around the world had three common characteristics: they had an intimate, conscious relationship with their place; they were stable 'sustainable' cultures, often lasting for thousands of years; and they had a rich ceremonial and ritual life. They saw these three as intimately connected."

—Dolores LaChapelle,
*Art and Ceremony in
Sustainable Culture*

The Physical World/Manifestation

Rituals can be of great assistance in dealing with difficult situations in the physical world. Such changes might include moving to another state, being put on a strict diet by your doctor, recognizing physical limitations, or turning a particular age. In Chapter 4: The Process of Ritual, we describe a ritual for a fortieth birthday to help you deal with dread, self-doubt, and the approach of middle age.

Ritual to Quit Smoking

After five years of smoking tobacco and three unsuccessful attempts at quitting, I decided a ritual was in order.

Preparation: On a brisk March day, carrying a knapsack with a canteen of water, an apple, journal and pen, matches, and my last two cigarettes, I hiked into the hills near my house. I traveled through parts of the woods I knew well, past the bog, and into new territory. As I scrambled over some rocks, a strong wind greeted me, and the sun shone warmly on my face. Looking at the inspiring view all around, I decided I had found the spot.

Manifestation: It was a small, private outcropping of rock and soil on the northern side of the hill. I walked around the space and found a comfortable place to sit and smoke my last cigarette. As I struck the match, I stated my *intention* that this would be the last cigarette I would ever need. While I smoked, I thought about all the times tobacco had been useful to me, how much I hated to give it up, and how it interfered with my life. I let these thoughts and feelings rise with the smoke.

Water from the canteen cleansed my mouth and throat and extinguished the cigarette, which I crumpled and buried in the dirt. I was, symbolically, quenching my need and burying my dependency. I stood holding the other cigarette high and asked aloud that the wind accept it as an offering, that Air assist me in not smoking. A gust of wind pulled the cigarette from my fingertips, and I inhaled the cold, clean air. I stated that whenever I needed to smoke, I would call on the wind to help me abstain. I then ate the apple to ground that promise. I gave thanks to Spirit for the wind, the sun, the water, the earth, and the tool of ritual.

Grounding: I wrote down the experience in my journal. On the way home, I buried the apple core at a place that seemed ready for an apple tree.

During the next few years, whenever I felt the desire for a smoke, I breathed deeply, or better yet, got a taste of the wind through a door or window. The fresh air filling my lungs, and the memory of the wind accepting my offering, was better than any cigarette could have been.

THE EMOTIONAL WORLD/DEEPENING

Use ritual to help you through difficult times. Dealing with depression is something that plagues us all now and then.

Ritual to Relieve Depression

We designed a ritual for a man who had felt depressed for several months after a job loss and was beginning to worry about himself.

Preparation: We instructed him to find a heavy overcoat and several layers of heavy clothing. On the overcoat, he was to pin slips of paper that named his bad feelings, such as "hopeless," "useless," "worthless," "apathetic," and so on. He also needed to come up with one thing about which he did not feel bad in his life. This turned out to be playing with his child.

Manifestation: On the day of the ritual, he woke up, darkened a room by drawing all the curtains, and donned all the heavy clothing, topped with the overcoat. Then, for no less than thirty minutes, he was really to get into moping, dragging around, or lying moaning on the floor. He pulled one slip of paper from the coat at a time and got really involved with that feeling. After he went through all the papers, he crumpled them up and burned them in a safe container, saying good-bye to each one. Then he took off the coat and all the clothes, opened the curtains, and went into the bathroom to shower, shave, and dress in something he really liked. After he dressed, he took his child to the zoo for the afternoon and did not return until he was sure they'd both had a very good time.

Grounding: When they arrived back home, it was to a surprise dinner his wife had prepared. Attempting humor, she had made a dinner using mostly "light" foods. He later reported that his depression had lifted considerably.

THE MENTAL WORLD/RELATEDNESS

When you are working on a project and feel "stuck," ritual can help you move beyond it. Use ritual to help you open up to artistic inspiration or to clarify and deepen your creative process.

Ritual to Prepare for Writing

Preparation: In writing this book, we used many rituals. To prepare myself for writing, I would first clean the room and gather my materials.

Manifestation: After lighting a candle, I walked to the east side of the room and asked Air for clarity of thought. Moving clockwise, to the south I asked Fire for the energy and inspiration necessary for the task. In the west, my request to Water was for smoothness and depth of feeling and that I might be in touch with that which we all share. The north was the place to ask Earth for help getting my thoughts, feelings, and inspirations down on paper. After returning to the east to complete the circle, I returned to center, where my writing chair is, and asked for guidance, that the book be written to further the Divine Will.

Grounding: I gave thanks and began to write. This ritual helped me clear and focus myself. The writing that followed flowed much more easily—and needed fewer rewrites—than the work done without the ritual.

Ritual to Identify the Cause of an Obsession

Also use rituals to deal with obsessions. A ritual was designed for Neil, who developed an obsession with his new car. He realized things had gotten out of hand when he found himself going down to the parking lot to inspect his car every lunch hour and then washing it every afternoon when he arrived home from work.

Preparation: He wasn't sure if it was the car itself that meant so much to him or if some unknown feelings were manifesting symbolically. We decided on a ritual to help identify what was really going on. His ritual centered around a dialogue with the obsession.

Manifestation: At a selected time and place, he prepared to invoke the essence of his obsession and imagine it coming to life in a space a few feet before him. He treated this essence as if it were the genie that emerged from the bottle in the old fairy stories. He questioned it carefully and thoroughly and let the answers come to him. By the time he finished, he had come to realize that the car was such a major investment, he was not sure he had a right to it. He had to be careful to keep it in perfect condition, as if he had surreptitiously acquired it, and it might disappear or be taken away.

Grounding: With this realization, he was able to work with the connection between his image of himself and the symbol of the expensive new car and create more balance.

The Spiritual World/Initiation

Some people find that ritual is a beneficial form of spiritual practice. Meditation, contemplation, and prayer are all forms of practice that you might find useful at different times in your life, and you have probably found that one of these forms is more suited to your personal style than the others. In setting up a spiritual practice, it is important to work with a form that feels right to you and challenges you as well. If you are a deeply passionate person, for example, prayer may be second nature to you and the form you use most often. It would probably be useful for you to include a less emotional form of devotion in your practice as well, such as sitting meditation or contemplation, to help stir you out of imbedded personality patterns and create more balance in your life. Ritual can be useful in both of these endeavors.

A Ritual for Spiritual Practice

A friend of ours had been working on self-growth for several years and was anxious to incorporate new tools that would help her to be more consciously "on her path."

Preparation: One day after reading an article about the Goddess religion, she decided to look for ways to be more in harmony with the cycles of nature.

Manifestation: She decided to create a ritual to perform at each new and full moon. With the new moon symbolizing beginnings, she designed a ritual as a time for seeding plans for the month. In the full moon ritual, she let herself discover and give thanks for whatever she reaped that month. This included finding ways she had met and conquered challenges, as well as things that were obvious blessings.

Grounding: During the time between her two rituals, she worked on actualizing her plans and making use of the benefits and insights she gained from her ritual work.

Other people might prefer a daily practice. This could be as simple as lighting a candle and asking Spirit for balance in body, feeling, mind, and soul as you wait for the kettle to boil each morning. It is simple to do and a fine way to start the day. You can certainly use more elaborate rituals—similar to the circle described earlier in this chapter in the ritual to prepare for writing—but when beginning a practice, a ritual that is not too complex works best. Over time, the morning candle ritual brings much more balance into your life and increased awareness of Spirit throughout the day.

RITUALS IN RELATIONSHIPS

During your life, you are in different important one-to-one relationships. You are a friend, a child, a lover, a parent, or perhaps a business partner. In this section, we discuss how to use ritual to honor and assist changes that occur in such relationships.

THE PHYSICAL WORLD/MANIFESTATION

We have cultural rituals for weddings, and we celebrate anniversaries, but we could also use ritual to honor a new partnership or a deepening of commitment between friends. We can also use ritual to help resolve problems in relationships and strengthen our bonds.

A good relationship is built actively and over time. When two people get together, no matter how compatible they are, important differences will exist between them. Sometimes we assume we understand someone's behavior when we are only interpreting it through our own filters.

A Ritual for Business Relationships

Two business partners who began a new venture found themselves faced with misunderstandings of each other's actions and moods.

Preparation: They developed a ritual based on role reversal to help them understand how each perceived the other.

Manifestation: Using this theme, they agreed to spend an entire day in the emotional and behavioral role of the other, acting as they felt the other acted.

Grounding: Afterward, they processed what came up for each of them and found out that they both shared fears about their new venture they thought the other did not have. They were then able to get back in sync with each other and work effectively.

THE EMOTIONAL WORLD/DEEPENING

Ending relationships is usually difficult. A ritual may be able to help the individuals involved honor the love and relatedness they had in the past and help the healing begin.

Ending Ritual for a Relationship

Two friends of ours decided to separate after being together for three years.. Couples counseling helped them recognize that they still loved each other, but they had grown in different ways. Their old relationship no longer suited either of them, and to keep it up would only lead to fights and pain. They wanted to remain friends, but did not know how to let go of their past way of relating. We helped them develop the following ritual.

Preparation: After planning and preparing, they drove to the country, riding around until they found an appropriate place.

Manifestation: They dug a hole and placed some artifacts of their relationship in it—a few gifts, a letter, a shared pillowcase. During the week, Tom wrote a poem and Jean made a picture, symbolizing the significance of what they previously had together. They shared these creations with each other and discovered they had each included what they had hoped the relationship would become.

Together they put the drawing and poem into the hole and set them on fire. They acknowledged these symbols of their past and of their hopes and let their desires and their old form of relating pass away as the papers burned.

Grounding: When the fire burned out, they covered it with dirt and planted flowers over the remains of their old relationship. As they watered the flowers, they said a prayer that what had died could find life in a new and better form. They then held each other and wept together, glad that they did not have to go through this ending alone.

A few months after this ritual took place, Jean and Tom found they were able to become friends, even though it was a bit awkward at first. Their relationship changed and grew, as did they.

The Mental World/Relatedness

A pair of friends were both going through stressful periods in their lives and found that when they got together, they often ended up commiserating with each other, rather than doing the creative projects that were so nourishing to them and their relationship.

A Ritual for Healing Friendship

Preparation: They chose to integrate a "worry box" into a healing ritual for themselves. They each wrote of their worries for themselves and their relationship on separate cards, including the reason for the concern, the worst fear, and how far inside or outside of their range of control the worry was. An example of this would be worrying about making a deadline versus whether or not a major earthquake would occur. They placed the cards in a box and designated certain times when they met to worry—the ten minutes after their first cup of coffee together.

Manifestation: They worried as much as they could during the specified time, but when worries came up later in their conversation, they reminded themselves to wait until the next worry period and got involved with a project instead.

Grounding: They noticed that they often found solutions to their concerns at the end of the worry periods and were able to come up with creative ways to implement those solutions.

THE SPIRITUAL WORLD/INITIATION

A couple we know was very happy together. Their only area of contention was in recurrent arguments over religious matters. Each was very devoted spiritually, but to two significantly different paths. They devised a ritual to help them better understand the other's views and beliefs and to transcend the different forms of the Spirit from whence each form was created.

A Ritual for Spiritual Understanding

Preparation: Both took time to look more deeply at their chosen paths in terms of the archetypes of the Elements, the types of rituals used in their systems, and basic tenets of the path. Together they built an altar with symbols from both paths in each quadrant.

Manifestation: During the ritual, they explained to each other the meaning of their symbols and their celebrations, noting how they were different from yet similar to each other. This led them to an exploration of the nature of Essence and how each path worked for each individual with their different styles of being in the world.

Grounding: They sat quietly and meditated on what they learned, not only about the other's system and self, but also about their own path and person and the meaning and presence of Spirit. To ground this process, they presented each other with gifts they chose in the other's symbolic system as a gesture of support and understanding.

FAMILY RITUALS

Rituals come naturally to families. This section covers how to improve and deepen rituals that are already present in a family, as well as other applications of ritual in family life. Changing residences or buying a summer cottage or a new family car can be times for celebration and are times to honor change.

THE PHYSICAL WORLD/MANIFESTATION

My friend Sue; her eight-year-old son, Terry; and Sue's boyfriend, Steven, were moving into their new house! They wanted a ritual that would cleanse the feeling of previous tenants and welcome them into their new home, a place of nurturance, support, happiness, and growth. While Sue and Steven had been in a relationship for a fair amount of time, this was the first time they would live together as a family, so it was also important that the ritual honor this commitment and generate energy for their family as a unit.

New House Ritual

Preparation: A few friends gathered and enlisted Terry's aid in making candleholders from aluminum foil. The adults enjoyed his creations, and he helped us place one in each room.

Manifestation: Everyone gathered in the kitchen—the heart of the house. After stating the *intention* and the opening prayers, the adults set out. We took bells and drums and, burning sage throughout the house and around the property, made quite a racket to clear out the old energy. Terry thought we were all a bit loony and watched us with puzzled amusement. When we went through the house a second time, saying a blessing in each room, Terry joined us. His chosen task was to light each candle with a large wooden fireplace match.

Grounding: We ended the ritual with a wine blessing. Each guest poured wine into a cup as they expressed their wishes for Terry, Steven, and Sue. The family poured some of the wine onto the earth, to symbolize sharing their blessings, and drank the rest to "digest" the good wishes. The three placed the gift of a triple-joined crystal on the mantelpiece in recognition of their unity. They had joined together and made the house truly theirs.

THE EMOTIONAL WORLD/DEEPENING

Families support each member in dealing with individual difficulties, disappointments, and losses. Families also celebrate the success of the individual members, be it getting a new job, being awarded a scholarship, or winning a race or a spelling bee.

To celebrate an important event in my family, we made a toast using special blue-and-white glasses. My father was a glassblower and made a personalized glass for each of us. We only used the glasses at very meaningful times, and we recorded the event on a piece of paper kept with the glasses in their own box. The toast always preceded a specially cooked dinner that we ate by candlelight in the warmth of our happiness and unity. This was a simple ritual, but one that touched us all deeply.

THE MENTAL WORLD/RELATEDNESS

Power struggles in a family can severely undermine the love and security for which we rely on families. The Taylor family ran into trouble when a job transfer prompted a move to another city. The two children, aged twelve and fourteen, felt betrayed and manipulated and decided to fight back. The key to a successful ritual in this case was to create a situation in which the children could feel that their lives, including their wants and needs, were as important as those of their parents. To accomplish this, the children were permitted to plan a farewell party for friends of the entire family.

As each individual grows through life, families are affected by these passages. Ritual can help ease the transitions of starting school, reaching puberty, retirement, and menopause. The form of the family changes as well. There are births and adoptions, divorces, the blending of two families in marriage, the death of a family member or a family pet, children moving out, children growing up, and sons- and daughters-in-law to welcome. Rituals can be valuable in supporting all these changes.

The Spiritual World/Initiation

Anniversaries, birthdays, and holidays are examples of cyclical rituals in families. Also create rituals for the single purpose of celebrating the love that exists in the family. Doing so honors and deepens the family bonds and each individual's sense of belonging.

Family Dinner Ritual

If you have Sunday family dinners, choose one Sunday a month for a ritual dinner. The Sunday closest to the new moon is a good time to sow the emotional and energetic seeds you would like to see grow and bloom in the coming month.

Preparation: Preparing the dinner can be a group endeavor, taking special care in setting the table to inspire beauty, harmony, and union.

Manifestation: Before soup or salad, each person individually thanks each of the family members for something he or she has done in the past month that benefited the family. Prior to the main course, each member thanks the others for personal qualities that they possess and that are appreciated. Before dessert, everyone states something about themselves that they like. Following dessert, each person names a quality of the family that is precious to them, that helps them in their life, and that they would like to receive more of in the coming month.

Grounding: In the coming month, each person can remember and act on the qualities named during the ritual. When such seeds are sown in love, they are sure to flourish.

GROUP RITUALS

Clubs, school classes, businesses, sports teams, and musical bands are some groups that can benefit from ritual. While these groups form for different purposes, they all move through some similar transitions, which are related to those discussed in the previous section on families.

THE PHYSICAL WORLD/MANIFESTATION

Families who have come to know each other over the years no longer make up neighborhoods. On many blocks, there are so many units with people coming and going after only a short time that many neighbors do not even recognize one another. The crime rate in cities is increasing rapidly, so on some blocks, the residents have found home alert meetings to be useful. A representative from the police department comes to one of the homes, where all the interested neighbors gather, and they discuss safety measures and agree to watch out for one another. This ritual-like situation can be enhanced by the neighbors having a kind of block party. In addition to socializing and discussing safety, they can also work on networking or creating a skill bank or job core. This can include babysitting, recycling, gardening, hauling, and other things that some neighbors may need and others may be able to provide.

THE EMOTIONAL WORLD/DEEPENING

Group rituals can support group members in their individual transitions as well.

"When words are inadequate, ceremony and ritual help us express our profound thoughts and feelings...rituals are symbolic activities that help us, together with our families and friends, express our deepest thoughts and feelings about life's most important events."

— Dr. Alan Wolfelt,
    Director of the Center
    for Loss and Life Transition

A Wedding Ritual

Preparation: If one of your women friends is getting married and doesn't need or care for the gifts from a traditional bridal shower, give her a ritual bridal shower. As part of the ritual, each of the bride's women friends brings a present representing a different aspect of being a woman.

Manifestation: For the "little girl," a book of fairy tales and a jar of bubbles would be appropriate. Someone might give a negligee to honor the "temptress/lover" aspect of the feminine or a crystal pendant and a journal to keep her in touch with her "wise old woman." A golden paper crown can celebrate the "queen of the realm" of the household, and could be followed by the gift of a pillow, on which the queen could rest her weary head after a day of toil. At the end of the ritual, all the participants may well feel full and powerful.

Grounding: The bride should bring herself to her wedding day with the aspects of the feminine whole balanced within.

THE MENTAL WORLD/RELATEDNESS

Many groups form around creative projects. The alignment of a group for a specific purpose is in itself such a creative project, and many groups use ritualized behavior to gather and focus their energy.

Before a big football game, pep rallies and pep talks occur in the locker room. The team forms a circle to raise their energy and unite them before they charge onto the field. This ritual action might be made even more effective with the conscious intention of the team members doing their best, both individually and collectively, and focusing less on beating the other team.

A singing group entering a competition could use a ritual to help them align with one another and sing better than ever before. While this could involve a complex ritual, it could also be as simple as the group forming a circle, holding hands, focusing their intention, and chanting "Om" together, as a means of aligning themselves while increasing their consciousness and skill.

THE SPIRITUAL WORLD/INITIATION

As well as needing alignment to purpose, a group can need healing. Whether it be poor communication, general grumblings of dissatisfaction, or a budget crisis, a group can benefit from dealing with its problems in the realm of Spirit as well as in the arena of practical problem-solving.

One way to approach this is to offer a healing circle at the end of community meetings after attending to business. Those who wish to participate can join in a circle and clear themselves from heavy concerns by concentrating on their breath and filling themselves with light. By imagining the light of the individuals blending, participants can get in touch with their relationships with one another and with the group and can also get a clearer sense of the community energy or group soul. Similar to the ritual for planetary healing in Chapter 3: Types of Rituals, the community members imagine the wounds of the group healing and ask the group soul or higher powers to fill the entire organization with light and wellness. This unites the community and enables Spirit to help smooth and guide the way through difficulties.

Small Community Ritual to Begin Healing after Trauma

On the morning of 9/11, shocked and scared, like all of us, I arrived at work. My four codirectors and I were glad to be together and relieved that most everyone we knew was safe. Our main concern was our students, who would arrive within the hour. Contra Costa Alternative School is small, with a maximum of forty students, and we weren't sure how many would show up that day, but we knew we all needed to come together as a community.

Preparation: The teenagers wandered in alone or in small groups. By quarter past the hour, about twenty-five were there, and we gathered them and all of the staff in the lounge. We updated the students on the news they might have missed in transit and explained our intention and our plan for the day to the students. Because of the shocking events of the morning, we would do a Go-'Round. (We always do Go-'Rounds whenever an issue affects the whole school community, and we knew its familiarity would comfort the group.) Each of us would have a chance to say as much or as little as we wanted to, about how we felt, what we were thinking, and/or what we needed. When one person finished, the next person would speak. We would keep going around the circle until everyone had said whatever he or she needed to say. People could address what another person had said, but only during their individual turns. The only rules were to be respectful and not to interrupt one another.

We also asked that each of us check in about people we cared about: did we know if they safe or where they were? What information or resources did we need? Did students need the structure of school or to go home? And we began the Go-'Round.

Manifestation: Two of the directors spoke first, as a way to model expressing difficult, and often conflicting, emotions. As we went around the circle, a huge range of emotions and attitudes was given voice: confusion, numbness, anger, fear, dread, compassion, sorrow, stoicism, shock-induced apathy, isolation, and helplessness. There was little vitriol, and a lot of tears, especially for friends and relatives who lived or worked near Ground Zero and whose fate was unknown. Virtually everyone told the story of first finding out about the news: where they were, what they were doing, what they heard and felt. Telling our stories was important in making the events real and starting to integrate the information and emotional impact. Every trauma victim needs to tell his or her story and keep telling it until the telling is done. Having your story witnessed in a group, and hearing everyone else telling their stories, can help the process along.

By the end of the second round, participants began expressing thankfulness for the community and amazement that such deep feelings—and some very opposite and strongly held political convictions—were given voice and were heard and respected. By the end of the third round, we had all had our say and did a simple healing circle.

Thank you all for being here today as part of this community; for coming together and sharing your experiences with each other; we are all the richer for it and comforted by it. As we sit in this circle, may we all become even more aware of this feeling of community, how it connects us, and makes us stronger than we could be on our own. Let us become aware of how this heartfelt energy connects us with the greater energy of Spirit and how that healing energy surrounds us and fills us. Let us imagine this healing energy concentrated in the center of our circle, and imagine those people we love held within this energy.... Now imagine this healing energy getting stronger and helping those people most affected by this tragedy: the victims of today's attack, their families and loved ones, their rescuers, those people so warped with pain and fear they would commit such acts, and our world leaders who need to respond wisely. We send this healing energy to wherever it is most needed in the world.

Grounding: We put our hands toward the center of the circle, palms up, and symbolically lifted the energy up and released it. We acknowledged that our need to be of help might be very great and that helping could be very healing. The Red Cross was asking for blood donations, which we mentioned; many teens could help in other ways—all kinds of community services needed help—and we suggested to the students that helping anywhere would add to the connectedness and healing that were so needed. Most people hugged. The directors made sure the students had people at home to be with them, and the staff took home those students who didn't have rides.

The next day we did another Go-'Round, which was especially important for students who were absent for the first one. After the Go-'Round, we went back to our regular Wednesday schedule, which students and staff felt would be best for reclaiming a sense of stability amidst the chaos.

This chapter gives you examples of different ways to use rituals, individually, in relationships, and with family and community. The self-exploration questions below can help you find rituals that directly relate to your life now.

SELF EXPLORATION

During the week, consider how to use what you have learned.

1. At present, or in the near future, where could you use an individual ritual?

   A relationship ritual?

   A family ritual?

   A group ritual?

2. Choose one type of ritual, and jot down some notes for developing the ritual.

conclusion

In a ritual, each object, action, or word has mythic significance. We have found that ritual reminds us that in normal life, this is also true—a concept we tend to forget when we get caught up in the compelling lure of form and accomplishment. The hunger for value so prevalent in our society illuminates the need to recognize the power in conscious awareness, in purposeful action. Life is not meaningless unless we do not attend to the meaning inherent in existence. The sacred is always present, always available. We need only remember to step back from the bustle and drudgery of daily life to receive it.

Ritual is a tool to focus our attention on meaning; we can develop this skill to enhance each moment of our lives. To be truly present in our own lives is an ability we must develop to continue building a foundation of relatedness and beauty in a world that can seem so divided and in pain. The new paradigm of wholism has been embraced increasingly over the last twenty years and is being felt on all levels of reality. This book is a manifestation of that growth, and we hope it serves the purpose of allowing more light, joy, meaning, and sacredness into your life.

This book presents you with the facets and process common to rituals, different types of rituals, and examples of ways to apply them. By now your awareness and understanding are likely to have shifted, even

"In order to arrive there,
To arrive where you are, to get from where you are not,
You must go by a way wherein there is no ecstasy.
In order to arrive at what you do not know
You must go by a way which is the way of ignorance.
In order to possess what you do not possess
You must go by the way of dispossession.
In order to arrive at what you are not
You must go through the way in which you are not.
And what you do not know is the only thing you know
And what you own is what you do not own
And where you are is where you are not."

—T. S. Eliot,
Four Quartets

169

if you have not yet begun to practice the art of ritual. Appendix A contains a recap of some of the primary ideas about which you have read. You may be surprised at how much seems familiar.

SELF EXPLORATION

Take the time to reread all your notes.

1. How do you feel you have changed since starting this journey?

2. How has your ritual work affected you in your transition?

3. What questions about creating rituals do you have now? Where can you get help with these questions? With whom can you discuss them?

4. Evaluation: Your feedback is important to us. What parts of the book worked best for you? What parts were the most difficult? Can you explain why? What suggestions do you have for improving the book?

5. Would you be interested in individual or group consultations or trainings in ritual from the authors?

6. What other subjects would you like to see us offer in training or in books?

We welcome your evaluation of *The Art of Ritual*. **Email Renee at dreamcrucible@hotmail.com, or send mail to her at CCAS, 10 Irwin Way, Orinda, CA 94563. Contact Sydney at doctorsydney@yahoo.com.**

We appreciate your time and energy. The work you are doing is important in bringing balance and healing to yourself and to our world.

APPENDIX A

elemental correspondences

By now you probably feel comfortable with the concept of the four Elements—Fire, Air, Water, and Earth—and perhaps you are beginning to relate these Elements to different parts of your daily life. By doing so, you increase the sense of the sacred in yourself and your world. To help you in that endeavor, the following is a chart of some possible correspondences to the Elements, including how the Elements relate to different kinds of rituals, the ritual process, and applications.

ELEMENT	FIRE	AIR	WATER	EARTH
Symbol	Flames	Bell, Incense	Cup	Disc, Cube
Color	Red	Blue	Silver	Earth Tones
Geometry	Point	Line	Plane	Solid
State of Matter	Combustion	Gas	Liquid	Solid
Personal Facet	Energy	Mind	Feeling	Body
Aspect of Relationships	Passion	Communication	Emotion	Affection
Learning	Desire	Study	Integration	Application
Creativity	Inspiration	Planning	Process	Product
RITUALS				
Type	Beginning	Merging	Cycle	Ending
World	Inspiration Energy	Creation Mental	Deepening Feeling	Manifestation Action
Application	Individual	Relationships	Family	Group

THE PROCESS OF RITUAL

PREPARATION

△ Fire: Intention
△ Air: Planning
▽ Water: Emotional Process
▽ Earth: Physical Preparation

MANIFESTATION

▽ Earth: Creating a Sacred Space
▽ Water: Setting the Mood
△ Air: Declaring the Intention
△ Fire: Invocation
△ Air: Direction of Higher Energies
▽ Water: Blessing
▽ Earth: Closure

GROUNDING

▽ Earth: Breakdown of Sacred Space
▽ Water: Emotional Process
△ Air: Evaluation
△ Fire: Integration

APPENDIX B

the rite of spring

This section is composed of two complete rituals created to welcome spring and all the season symbolically implies. You can do the first ritual alone or as the individual prelude to the second ritual, which also honors spring, but is designed for a group. Both the individual and group ritual follow the steps outlined in Chapter 4: The Process of Ritual.

Feel free to use one or both of these rituals for yourself. Follow them directly or modify them to suit your needs.

RITUAL FOR INDIVIDUAL EXPRESSION

PREPARATION

Begin by clarifying your intention. Step one: It is spring, either by the calendar or by the weather. The changing of the seasons offers an excellent opportunity for a cyclical celebration. In some traditions in which ritual has a large role, such as the shamanic or

Wiccan ones, aligning your inner world with the greater cycles of the earth is a powerful way to achieve both inner balance and understanding of the rhythm of change.

What happens in the outer world, in nature, during spring? During this season, we see the gray, solemn mantle of winter burst into life. Spring is the time of rebirth and new beginnings. It holds a sense of possibility, hope, vitality, and release. Spring is not only a cyclical celebration, but also a beginning. In many ways, it is appropriate to think of spring, or the spring equinox, as the beginning of the year.

If you reflect on all the outer world associations for spring, you can then move on to step two in the planning process. If you would like to perform a ritual for yourself, focus on bringing yourself out from the constraints of winter. This release needs time to take hold. For this ritual, you will be involved in a process that unfolds over four to seven days. Each day will include a few short periods of time spent cleansing, releasing, and reflecting. This culminates in a ceremony that takes about an hour. This sequence, which leads you through a gradual awakening, is much like the transformation from caterpillar through chrysalis to butterfly. It teaches you, among other things, about the patience you need to develop to allow growth to occur. You can do the whole ritual process right in your kitchen. If you have a yard or access to a private natural area, you may want to do the ceremony outdoors.

PLANNING

Now that you have clarified the intention, assemble the symbolic Elements you require. Gather seeds for sprouting, edible wild plants and flowers, if available, salad ingredients, and a table for an altar. These all represent the Element of Earth. For the Element of Air, you need a journal for writing the thoughts and feelings that arise and also some labels for the jars. The water used for washing and soaking seeds, the quart jars for sprouting, and a bowl for a salad represent the Element of Water. You use a large candle, representing Fire, in the invocation of the energy of spring. Also, you need a box of small candles (birthday candles would be appropriate) to connect with the inspiration and higher guidance that Fire represents. Finally, Essence, the unifying Element, is represented by the sunlight, as well as by the tone that must constantly be present, almost as a mantra, that says, "The outer reflects the inner world; the inner world resonates in harmony with the outer."

EMOTIONAL PROCESS

As we stated before, this is a process ritual, one of gradual awakening. Spending time with your thoughts and feelings each day is part of the transformation facilitated by this ritual. Think of the physical steps taken throughout the ritual as mirrors, reflecting the feelings you are experiencing with your own cleansing and growth.

PHYSICAL PREPARATION

These are the steps of the daily ritual: choose one or more personal goals that you are working on "giving birth to," such as setting priorities, improving communication in a relationship, or getting into shape. Or choose something you are working on letting go of: for example, anxiety, depression, or procrastination. Match one of these with one of the types of seeds you chose for sprouting. You might choose alfalfa seeds to denote procrastination and radish seeds to represent improving the way you would like to communicate in a relationship.

Make a label naming each goal you developed. Put a handful of seeds in a quart jar with a screen or cheesecloth top. Label each jar with the goal that the seeds within represent. Pour enough water into each jar to cover the seeds, and leave them soaking overnight, imagining that as the seeds soak, so does the restrictive pattern of your "procrastination." For seeds to sprout, you must rinse and drain them twice a day. It would be advantageous to save the waters you use for rinsing in a large container. Between rinsings, rest the jars on their sides on a kitchen counter. Each time you are ready to wash the seeds, first light one of the small candles. Use this as a point of focus, inspiration, and connection with your source of higher guidance. Meditate on your issues, and attend to any sense of limitation that comes up around them. Use focusing questions such as, "What is my procrastination really about? How might procrastination be in some way a protection for me? What would my life be like if I did not avoid things I feel I should be doing?" Note in your journal both your thoughts and any feelings that arise during this process.

After a few days, the seeds will crack and sprouts will emerge. Continue your process, matching your inner pace to the changes in the seeds and recording your experience in your journal. When the sprouts grow to about an inch long, and when you get in touch with the sense of having grown in like manner, place the jar in the sun until the sprouts begin to green. The sun represents the energy of Essence. This symbolically calls for your growth to be recognized and nurtured by the Element of Essence as well.

Now your sprouts are ready for the culminating ceremony. This requires another physical preparation. For this part of the ritual, you need your sprouts and other ingredients with which to create a salad. If you live in or near a natural setting, you may want to take advantage of all the edible "weeds" that are so abundant in the spring, such as miner's lettuce, chickweed, or dandelion greens. Symbolically, this is a way of saying that even what seem to be weeds—obstacles or useless materials—can really be nurturing and even medicinal! Also, many plants have edible flowers; nasturtiums are one of the most popular. Filling your salad with spring flowers is like filling your bowl with beauty and the life force that manifests in the outer world in spring.

To create your altar, find a table you can bring to the ritual setting. Transform a table into an altar by first covering it with some special fabric, a tablecloth, or a scarf. (See Chapter 7: Altars for more information on erecting altars.) Fill a vase with some spring flowers, and place it on the altar. Find a large white candle and candleholder. White candles are commonly used to represent the Element of Essence, as white is the blend of all colors. Bring other items that symbolize spring for you or any "power objects" you may have (Chapter 6: Crafting and Consecrating Tools gives details on making ritual tools) to place on or around the altar to help personalize the ritual. You need the container of water you saved from rinsing the seeds, particularly if you will perform the ritual outdoors. And, of course, you need your journal.

Before you begin the next part of the ritual, set aside an uninterrupted block of time to prepare, perform, and complete the process. As you will transform the ritual site into a sacred space, it is essential that the site be a place you feel assured will be private. Whatever you can do beforehand to bring forth that consecrated feeling is important. If you perform the ceremony in your kitchen, it would be helpful to clean and straighten it thoroughly. If you are outdoors, you may wish to somehow mark and clear a circle in which you feel the energy to be different within than without. It is also crucial to prepare yourself. This is, after all, a celebration of personal transformation; something in you is changing. You will want to bathe, perhaps with flowers, oils, or bubbles. Choose clothing that makes you feel special. You may want to decorate yourself in some way, possibly with face paint or other ornamentation.

MANIFESTATION

This is the enactment of the rite. Creating a sacred space can be the first ceremonial performed act. Consecrating and arranging your altar may be your first areas of focus. After arranging the altar, some people like to cleanse and anoint their tools. Cleanse energetically with a sprinkling of salt or saltwater, with smudging (passing burning herbs or incense over), or any other way that suits you. Anoint with scented waters or oils (see Chapter 6: Crafting and Consecrating Tools). You can also smudge or otherwise cleanse the ritual space. After setting everything in your circle, step outside of it. Stand at the edge or entrance to the space, and take in the scene. Know that you are about to enter another world, a world that can be as magical as the world of your dreams and imagination. Pass the burning incense around yourself, allowing the smoke to clear away any doubts or fears. Take three deep, full breaths. With each breath, inhale a feeling of the extraordinary and exhale the ordinary. Step into the circle.

DECLARATION AND ENACTMENT OF INTENTION

Kneel before your altar. Light and raise the candle. State that you are there to honor spring, birth, beginnings, growth, release, and energy.

Invocation of Larger Energies

Ask that the essence of spring be present for you during the ritual. Ask that you may feel the qualities of spring alive in you to support and assist your own inner spring and sense of rebirth. Return the candle to the altar. You may want to put your hand on each item to enhance your connection with what they represent. Sit with your journal, and read through the notes from the past several days. Allow time to access and experience whatever feelings you may associate with your entries.

Take the ingredients for your salad. Meditate on what each item in your bowl means to you. Ask that your food be blessed and that it bring you strength to further your growth. Eat your salad, savoring the attention, care, and development it embodies.

When you finish, pour the seed water into your bowl. Carry the water to a plant or place on the ground to pour it. As you give the water back to the Earth, let it be an offering to nourish the growth of other plants and a gift of gratitude to nature for its gifts.

Blessing and Closure

Return to the altar. With the candle, walk clockwise around the circle or kitchen, thanking the essence of spring for attending your ritual, and allow this essence to withdraw. Placing the candle back on the altar, wet your fingers and snuff the flame.

Grounding

The ceremony is complete.

BREAKDOWN
Carefully and thoughtfully return everything to its appropriate place or condition.

EVALUATION
As you do this, consider what occurred over the past several days. Are you satisfied with the process that transpired? Would you add or delete anything if you were to do it again? How do you think you may have benefited from this ritual?

INTEGRATION AND ACTUALIZATION
In the following days, look for instances that show how your behavior has shifted. Notice if you seem to have more choices or a greater sense of freedom. Record your observations in your journal. Remind yourself of this ritual process whenever you are in a situation that involves your particular area of personal growth. Some of these changes may be subtle; you may notice others only after a period of time passes. Be gentle with yourself and grateful for what has occurred.

You may want to celebrate the arrival of spring with your friends. The following ritual is designed for a group of five to twenty people, and the ceremony itself takes approximately forty-five minutes. The plan is presented with you as the facilitator or coordinator, but you may want to work closely with a few of your friends or colleagues throughout the preparation stages as well as during the ritual.

RITUAL FOR GROUP EXPRESSION

PREPARATION

In the individual ritual for spring, we discussed the emergence of life and new growth. Spring is the time of year when bulbs planted in the fall struggle through the earth to reach the air and light. Traditionally in Western religions, it is a time of sacrifice and rebirth into a greater sense of freedom. At Passover, a lamb was sacrificed so the firstborn sons could live. This led to the Exodus of the Jewish tribes to a new land as a free people. Christians celebrate Good Friday and Easter, when Jesus was crucified and resurrected. In this act, the Christ offered freedom to the souls of humanity as well as the keys to eternal life.

CLARIFYING THE INTENTION

Following this theme, the intention of this ritual is to honor the inspirations gestating in each of us, to recognize and release the aspects of ourselves that impede the birth of these inspirations, and to create ways to consciously help those inspirations grow in ourselves and in the world.

PLANNING

Although we present a complete ritual, you might want to take the time to allow the expression of your own unique creation. Consider what kind of actions might represent gestation, struggle, sacrifice, and creation. How might you arrange the ritual space to represent these stages? Note your ideas and make a basic outline.

Each Element must be represented in the ritual. While writing your plan, you probably included some of them. Check to make sure all are present. As you do so, your plan will continue to develop. We selected the following Elemental representations for this ritual:

Earth ▽ *The hibachi or brazier containing the central fire represents the winter earth holding the inspiration about to be born. Use husks, shells, or some facsimile as a physical token of a protection no longer needed. To symbolize gestation, darken the room, with the group sitting or squatting in it. The sprouts that you and your friends have nurtured and brought represent the ways each of you has grown, and eating the salad signifies incorporating these qualities. Ask each person to bring a small gift that exemplifies what they feel is being born in them. The giving of the gift helps that new quality find a place in the world.*

Water ▽ *Illustrate growth with movements, such as stretching or unfolding, or even more simply with something to drink. As you celebrate the increase of light, you may want to try orange juice with a little grenadine at the bottom—a sunrise.*

Air △ *When each member is ready to sacrifice a certain quality or way of being to the fire, he or she can state that quality while putting a slip of paper naming the quality into the flames. After the sacrifice, the participants can create something by writing or drawing, or perhaps they can develop a group poem or story to express the release of inspiration.*

Fire △ *The Element of Fire symbolizes inspiration, and you can use a small central fire (in a brazier, hibachi, or some safe space outdoors; or simply an incense charcoal indoors) to represent this. Use this fire to help "burn away" whatever the participants need to sacrifice to let their inspirations emerge.*

Essence ☉ *The light from the central fire is the fount that draws and unites the participants in their darkness. After the sacrifice, draw back the curtains or turn on the lights, as the participants come to the light of conscious awareness. Essence nourishes the soul as the sunlight vitalized the seedlings. An invocation of Spirit at the beginning and a giving of thanks at the end of the ritual also acknowledge Essence. Another option is having the group clasp hands in a circle, the symbol for unity.*

Now consider logistics, in which you get down to details. The easiest way to cover all the bases is to use the journalist's formula of who, what, when, where, and why.

* *Why* is covered in the section on clarifying your intention, so move on to the other categories.

* *Who* will be involved in the ritual? As you list the potential participants, consider if the ritual as it is planned will offend anyone. If children will be involved, will the ritual be short enough to hold their attention and simple enough for them to understand?

During this phase of the planning, you need to delegate responsibilities. Who will gather what materials, set up, perform what stage of the ritual, do the cleanup, and so forth? Some of your friends may want to be involved in each stage of the ritual. Because the Elements are represented in many ways throughout the process, assigning each individual to carry out the functions of a particular Element would be one way to allocate duties. This gives the person in charge of Fire, for example, the responsibility of bringing the charcoal, hibachi, and matches. He or she would set the fire up, light it and tend it, and take it down at the end. This is a practical way of sharing the work, as well as enlivening a particular quality in the person with each assignment.

Throughout the rest of this ritual plan, you as coordinator represent Essence. Choose one person to take on the duties of each of the other four Elements.

* *What* do you need to do? What words do you need to speak? What order do you need to follow? Participants must be clear on how to prepare, what to bring, and what you expect them to do. You need to issue invitations. The following list gives you an idea of how to deter mine who can perform which tasks:

▽ Earth—bring food for a small salad, a salad bowl, and a tray; prepare a blessing for the salad.

▽ Water—bring orange juice, grenadine, clear plastic or glass cups; prepare a blessing to consecrate the drinks.

△ Air—make the invitations; bring light-colored construction paper, scissors, and a set of different colored felt-tipped markers; prepare a blessing to affirm the creativity that is given its freedom during the ceremony.

△ Fire—bring a hibachi, a flat rock, a roll of incense charcoal, long matches, shaved cocoa shells, and a bowl to hold them; prepare a blessing for the fire.

⊙ Essence—bring a white candle, candleholder and matches, spirits for the drinks (*optional*); prepare opening and closing remarks; prepare to lead the ritual; coordinate.

* *When* includes not only the time the ritual will be held, but also the issuing of invitations, the gathering of ritual tools, and the time line of events in the ritual itself.

* *Where* will you hold the ritual? If it will be outdoors, will there be enough privacy? Does the area you chose allow you the opportunity to feel a sense of containment? Is there enough room for what you have planned? Determine where in the ritual space participants will enter, stand, and move. Where will you place altars or objects? Find specific directions for this later in the section on Manifestation, the ritual itself.

After you work out the logistics and choose the appropriate ritual Elements, it is time to go back to your basic idea and revamp it as needed. Plan out the ritual in sufficient detail, making notes about each step. As the coordinator, you need to know exactly what will happen during the ritual and be able to provide clear information to the other participants.

EMOTIONAL PROCESS
This is the time to check to see if you are remaining true to your intention and to note if you feel blocked in any way. More important, this is

when you want to sit down and gently consider whatever feelings are present about what has occurred. It is likely that some emotional issues will need your attention. Because you are in the position of Essence, you may find a resistance or hesitancy developing over the responsibilities of coordinating and helping the others stay in tune with the inspiration. Or you may find your ego becoming inflated with the power of your position. Whatever personal issues are revealed, now is the time to work through them.

Other issues or emotional struggles can occur in the relationships of the participants. Do any power struggles exist? Does anyone need more say in the *what* and *how* of the ritual process? Does anyone feel nervous or insecure about their role? Working on these interpersonal issues with a compassionate, creative, problem-solving approach will make the preparations go more smoothly and add depth to the ritual itself.

Responsibility is always the child of consciousness. While clarifying your intention for this ritual, you considered how the ritual would affect people. Having come this far in your preparation, it is important to address this issue again. You have gotten in touch with your issues and those of your friends. As you reflect on your intention and the ritual plan, can you discover if any possibility for harm or exclusion may exist that did not seem apparent before? If so, how can you best change this? As you grow on an ethical level, you replace walls with doors, each leading to opportunity.

PHYSICAL PREPARATION

The first aspect of this step is an extension of what you covered in logistics. Well before the day of the ritual, you issued invitations, made lists, and collected materials. Everyone knows what they need to do and is prepared to do it. While this ritual may not require a rehearsal, other rituals do and you would need to orchestrate that. After satisfactorily coordinating things, think about preparing yourself.

The individual ritual presented earlier is an excellent way to prepare for this group ritual. The outer self also needs preparation, and you may choose to fast or eat lightly the day of the ritual. Taking a bath in bubbles or oils and donning special clothing help create a kind of purification. You might also want to meditate on the intention, ask for higher guidance, and go over the ritual one more time before the others arrive.

Before you bathe and dress, you need to make ready the ritual space. Move the furniture as needed, dust, vacuum, and clean the space. For this ritual, in which Essence symbolically enters the gathering as light shining in through the windows, make sure the windows are clean and the curtains or shades open easily. After you complete the cleansing in the room and of yourself, return to the room to clear the space energetically. A simple way to do this is to stand in the center of the area facing east and light a candle to ask Spirit to help clear out all that does not harmonize with the purpose of the ceremony. Then, starting from the east and walking clockwise around the room, stop at each quadrant, asking for clarity of thought in the east, proper direction of energy from the south, emotional depth and compassion from the west, and groundedness and proper action from the north. Return to the east to complete the circle, then move to the center to thank Spirit for help in clearing the circle. Quietly leave the area.

Once your friends arrive with the items for the ritual, begin to set up. Water prepares a tray of sunrise drinks in the kitchen, and Earth creates a small salad. Air cuts egg shapes out of the construction paper.

Fire puts the shaved cocoa shells into a bowl. Draw the curtains and set a fire extinguisher outside the circle but close at hand. When everything is ready, you and Fire enter the ritual space respectfully. Help Fire set up the hibachi on a flat stone in the center of the circle, and Fire places the incense charcoal that she will later light in it. Each person in turn sets up the symbols of their Elements and quietly stands before them. Say a short blessing and thank the group for their work. All quietly leave the circle.

MANIFESTATION

Once you set up the space and the other guests arrive, guide them into the ritual circle around the hibachi. You and Water are in the west, in front of the sunrises. Earth is in the north, standing before the salad. Air stands in the east, pens and paper ready, and Fire is in the south with the bowl of cocoa shells. The other guests fill in the circle.

To begin you might say, "Welcome! Before we start, let's be silent for a moment, take a few deep breaths, and let go of any outer distractions we are holding. Allow yourself to feel the fondness we all have for one another and the caring and love that are present in this place today. We ask that the larger love as represented by the unity of Essence also be present here and that what we do today be guided by that force, that we may help ourselves and the world to be touched with love and light."

DECLARATION OF INTENTION

You may wish to talk about the feelings of coming through the winter months and beginning to experience the life associated with spring rising in us again. This dialogue can lead into the statement of intention:

"We ask that this ritual honor the inspirations gestating in us, that we may recognize and release that which impedes the birth of these inspirations in us, and that we can create ways for these inspirations to come to consciousness in ourselves and in the world." Clearly explain the phases of this ceremony, and ask the participants to sit or squat as a way of representing the dormancy of winter.

INVOCATION OF LARGER ENERGIES

Now Fire lights the central fire and speaks of the inner light kindled at the winter solstice, which has been gestating and is approaching the time of birth. Ask the participants to focus within on the power of this growth and to imagine trying to rise but being unable to do so: "What gets in your way? Seeds have to break through their shells to grow; what is *your* shell? What part of you, what quality, stops your growth right now? Allow a word, phrase, or image to come forth identifying this quality. Let yourself feel the limitations it imposes on you and also what your life could be like without it. Imagine how, free of this limitation, your inner spark would grow in the spring, take form during the summer, and come to full manifestation in the fall."

As you speak, Earth moves clockwise around the circle, giving each participant some cocoa shells. Instruct each person to come to the central fire when they are ready and speak the word that represents their limitation or shell over the cocoa shells, which they then sacrifice to the fire. After all members come forward and symbolically release that which hinders their growth, Fire can ask that Spirit accept these surrenderings and that the participants accept the truth that some quality that may have been an important part of their behavior can change.

As the sweet smoke of the burning shells rises upward, direct everyone to focus within and discover their feelings of constriction lifting and dispersing. Then, while all slowly rise, draw back the curtains, invoking the light and love and power of Essence to assist in recognition and acceptance of growth.

Everyone will stretch a bit, glad of the light and freedom. At this time, Air can walk clockwise around the circle, giving out pens and paper eggs. Explain that the eggs represent that which has been liberated. On the egg, each person is to draw symbols or pictures or write whatever they feel expresses this freedom. Earth goes around the circle again, this time holding a tray with the salad bowl. As everyone places the sprouts they grew in the past week in the bowl, they also put their eggs on the tray, speaking briefly of their release.

Earth then raises up the bowl and asks a blessing of Essence for the salad, to incorporate not only the inspirations just born, but also the presence and constancy of Spirit. Offer the salad to the group, and all partake of it.

Water then goes around the circle distributing the sunrise drinks. Everyone holds up the cup for a blessing as Water speaks of what is being symbolized. The blessing is made and everyone drinks. Next Air asks for a blessing for the paper eggs, that the experience they represent will be remembered. Each person then reclaims their egg.

Explain that the gifts represent what each person felt was to be born and they can now be passed on. As you give yours to the person on your left, speak briefly about the significance of your gift and, if you wish, how it relates to your experience in this ritual. Continue this process around the circle until the person on your right speaks and passes their gift to you.

Blessing and Closure

After collecting and setting the cups aside, all hold hands in a circle. Ask that everyone give thanks to themselves, to one another, and to Essence for the experience, the growth, and the togetherness. Also ask Spirit to help you bring the energy and consciousness gained during the rite into the world.

Grounding

The ritual is over, but before you and your friends begin to socialize, you must do a few things.

Breakdown

If any food that has been blessed is left over, you should consume it before you close the circle. Or you can save it and bury it. Pour any leftover drinks on the ground as a libation. The blessings made the food sacred, and it deserves respect.

To release the circle, you might stand in the center and say, "We thank thee, Spirit, for your presence here today. The work is done, and we release this sacred space to normal space," and clap your hands loudly. Extinguish the candle when clearing the space. Then break down the ritual setup, each person being in charge of their Element.

The circle breaks; people take their gifts and exit the space, going to another room to dance, talk, and celebrate the arrival of spring.

Emotional Process

During the party, note how you feel. You might find greater expression in your dancing or a fuller love for your friends. People will probably thank you for the ritual. It is likely that you will feel elation at successfully completing a large project, and it is important to remember that while you coordinated the ritual, the access to experiencing Essence permitted growth, change, and connection.

EVALUATION

Use the feedback from the people at the party and discussion with the core group to help you evaluate what worked well, what you could have done better, and how. Assess your work as coordinator and the effectiveness of the ritual as a whole. Add notes to the end of your ritual plan, so that if you perform this ritual again, you can improve it.

INTEGRATION AND ACTUALIZATION

Over the next week or so, be aware of how you access the inner change that occurred for you during the ritual. How do you bring it into the world? Look for opportunities to change old behavior patterns, and keep track in your journal of your emotional responses to these changes. Times may occur when you feel unable to change, to let go of the limitation of, for example, unreasonable fear, as you could do during the ritual. Remember that ritual is a powerful tool in creating change, but that change is still a gradual process, which takes time, energy, and courage. Call on Spirit and the power of the ritual experience to help you. When you receive help, give thanks.

Another way to help actualize the sense of inner release experienced in the ritual is to meet with your four friends to discuss how you all fared during this part of the process. As the group that created the ritual together, you have greater access to the energy of the ceremony than you have individually. Together brainstorm ideas for implementing change in your lives, and give each other perspective and support for your individual work. The group can also celebrate the steps toward growth taken by each of you. The unity and increased closeness of the group can remind you of your successful connection with Essence.

glossary

Air △ One of the Elements; a symbolic representation of the mind and thought, ideas, distinction, and understanding

altar A table or platform, usually raised, used in a sacred ceremony to hold offerings, power objects, or ritual items

archetype From Jungian psychology—an innate energy pattern of the psyche that is expressed symbolically

collective unconscious From Jungian psychology—the deepest layers of the unconscious, where memories and potentialities exist on a universal level and are available to everyone

Earth ▽ One of the Elements; a symbolic representation of that which is solid, tangible, has a sense of history, and provides support and practicality

Elements The archetypal substances that are the basic component parts or principles of any thing

Essence ⊙ The underlying and unifying nature of any thing; used as the fifth Element, bringing a sense of wholeness

fetish Something specially crafted to serve as a power object

Fire △ One of the Elements; a symbolic representation of passion, force, courage, vitality, and revolution or possibility

mythology The stories or legends of a people; the beliefs by which we live

numerology A numerical system used to help understand life; often applied to understanding personality characteristics

Ouroboros The snake biting its own tail; the Great Round, the eternal cyclicity

psyche An autonomous factor; the source of all human activities, being at once the conscious mind, the personal unconscious, and the collective unconscious

ritual A ceremony, particularly formalized, used to fulfill a certain intention

scrying Gazing into a reflective object to achieve insight or illumination

shamanism A spiritual practice that brings wisdom, healing, and change, based on the belief in the unity of all things and the honoring of all that is

Spirit Life force energy; the divine force

Tarot A set of seventy-eight cards, used primarily for self-understanding and also for understanding the larger relationships among self and others, others, and things as a whole

transpersonal Beyond the persona or mask; energy or awareness that transcends the personal

Water ▽ One of the Elements; a representation of feelings, sensitivity, and inner process

Wicca The old religion, the religion of the Great Goddess, a nature religion that honors the harmony and unity of all things

bibliography

Campbell, Joseph. *Myths to Live By.* New York: Arkana, 1993.

———. *The Power of Myth.* New York: Anchor Books, 1991.

Cirlot, J. E. *A Dictionary of Symbols.* New York: Dover Publications, 2002.

Eliade, Mircea. *Myths, Dreams, and Mysteries.* New York: Peter Smith Publishing, 1986.

Eliot, T. S. *Four Quartets.* New York: Harcourt, Brace, and World, 1971.

Fredman, N., and R. Sherwood. *Handbook of Structured Techniques in Marriage and Family Therapy.* New York: Brunner/Mazel, Inc., 1986.

Gray, William G. *The Ladder of Lights: A Step-by-Step Guide to the Tree of Life and the Four Worlds of the Qabalists Including the Angelic and Archangelic Realms.* Boston: Red Wheel/Weiser, 1994.

Halevi, Z'ev ben Shimon. *School of Kabbalah.* Boston: Red Wheel/Weiser, 1986.

Jung, C. G. *Analytical Psychology: Its Theory and Practice.* New York: Random House, 1968.

Malraux, André. *Les Métamorphoses des dieux*. In *The International Thesaurus of Quotations*, edited by Eugene H. Ehrlich. New York: HarperCollins, 1996.

Perls, Fritz. *The Gestalt Approach and Eye Witness to Therapy*. Ben Lomond, CA: Science and Behavior Books, 1973.

Ponce, Charles. *Kabbalah: An Introduction and Illumination for the World Today*. Madras, India: Theosophical Publishing House, 1978.

Sanford, John A. *Healing and Wholeness*. New York: Paulist Press, 1977.

Starhawk. *Dreaming the Dark: Magic, Sex, and Politics*. Boston: Beacon Press, 1997.

———. *The Spiral Dance: A Rebirth of the Ancient Religion of the Great Goddess*. San Francisco: HarperSF, 1999.

Van der Hart, Onno. *Rituals in Psychotherapy*. New York: Irvington Publishers, 1996.

Whitmont, Edward C. *Return of the Goddess*. London: Continuum Publishing Group, 1997.

Wilhelm, Richard. *I Ching*. New Jersey: Princeton University Press, 1967.

Woodman, Marion. *Addiction to Perfection: The Still Unravished Bride*. Toronto: Inner City Books, 1988.

about the authors

As a child, RENEE BECK led funerals for neighborhood pets; in high school she was introduced to the Tarot, and she has been working with ritual, dreams, energy, and symbolic systems ever since. A licensed marriage, family, and child therapist, she has a bachelor's degree in consciousness from Goddard College as well as master's degrees in transpersonal counseling and clinical psychology from John F. Kennedy University. She has worked at Contra Costa Alternative School since 1982, where she is a co-director and teacher who does

therapy with teenagers and their families and supervises counseling interns. She has a private practice in Transpersonal Dreamwork: Depth Therapy from the Soul, and offers consultation and training in ritual, Tarot, and related topics in the San Francisco Bay Area. You can reach Renee at dreamcrucible@hotmail.com.

SYDNEY BARBARA METRICK, Ph.D., has helped thousands of people make successful transitions in their lives. She has more than twenty years' experience in curriculum and program design. Her multidisciplinary background blends psychology, art, education, and business. Through training, teaching, counseling, and coaching, Sydney has helped individuals and groups develop skills, confidence, and success. Sydney is the author of three other books that address transitions, including *I Do: A Guide to Creating Your Own Unique Wedding Ceremony, Art from Ashes,* and *Crossing the Bridge.* She is a Certified Professional Co-Active Coach (CPCC) through the Coaches Training Institute and a Professional Certified Coach (PCC) through the International Coach Federation. You can reach Sydney at doctorsydney@yahoo.com.

index

cycle, 57
cyclical rituals
    altar for, 113–114, 117
    anniversaries as, 38
    associated with Water, 62
    celebration of, 43–48
    Elements in, 76, 78, 79
    function of, 53
    with others, 43
    spring ritual, group, 182–194
    spring ritual, individual, 174–181
    winter solstice ritual, 48–49

d

death, 49, 50, 51
depression, 149–150
Dias del los Muertos (Days of the
    Dead), 4–5
A Dictionary of Symbols (Cirlot), 82
dinner preparation ritual,
    58–59
dipped candles, 102–103
divorce, 154–155
divorce ritual, 51–53
Drawing on the Artist Within (Edwards),
    103–104
dream pillows, 98–99

e

Earth, Element of
    altar and, 114, 116
    associations of, 61, 80–81
    in cleansing, 105
    correspondences to, 75, 172
    defined, 195
    element selection guide for, 84
    relationship among, 74
    in ritual stages, 128
    in spring ritual, group, 183, 185,
        190, 191
    in spring ritual, individual, 175
earth mother, 28–29

eating, 30–31, 100, 180
Edwards, Betty, 103–104
Elements, 73–90
    altar types and, 111–115
    balance in, 73–74
    cleansing of tool with, 104–107
    correspondences to, 75, 171–172
    defined, 195
    described, 75–81
    element selection guide, 83–88
    journaling exercise for, 89–90
    mirror represents all, 103
    relationship among, 75
    in ritual stages, 127–128
    ritual types and, 37
    in spring ritual, 175–176, 182–186,
        188–191
    symbols, personalizing, 81–83
elevation, 109, 110
Eliade, Mircea, 33, 48
email address, 170
emotion, 50–51, 78–79
emotional process, 65–66, 176, 186–187,
    192–193
emotional world/deepening rituals,
    149–150, 154–155, 158–159,
    161–162
ending rituals
    altar for, 118–120
    divorce ritual, 51–53
    Elements in, 78, 79
    for end of relationship, 154–155
    function of, 53
    types of, 49–51
energies, 69, 112
energies, invocation of, 68, 179–180,
    190–191
energy, 62, 80–81
Erickson, Milton, 19–20
Essence, Element of
    altar types and, 111–112
    associations of, 62, 81–82

in cleansing, 105
defined, 196
element selection guide for, 88
represents unity, 75
in ritual stages, 128
in spring ritual, group, 184, 185, 186, 191
in spring ritual, individual, 176, 177, 178
evaluation, 70–71, 181, 193
An Explanatory Casebook (Erickson), 19–20

f

family rituals
    for adolescence, 40–43
    ritual altar for leaving home, 118–119
    symbols and, 82
    types of, 157–160
feelings, 78–79, 113–114, 126
fetish, 92, 93, 196
Fire, Element of
    altar and, 113–114, 115
    associations of, 62, 76–77
    in cleansing, 105
    correspondences to, 75, 172
    defined, 196
    element selection guide for, 87
    relationship among, 74
    in ritual stages, 128
    in spring ritual, 176, 184, 186, 190
Folklore, Mythology, and Legend (Funk and
    Wagnall), 32–33
friendship healing ritual, 155–156
Future Shock (Toffler), ix–x

g

Geertz, Clifford, 27
gifts
    in adolescence ritual, 42, 43
    in birthday ritual, 63
    in spring ritual, 183, 191
    in wedding ritual, 161–162
Goddess religion, 152–153
Great Goddess, 29